Ethics in Hedge Funds: Navigating the Moral Compass of Finance

Alex Thompson

Published by Side Hustle Success, 2023.

ETHICS IN HEDGE FUNDS: NAVIGATING THE MORAL COMPASS OF FINANCE

First edition. September 29, 2023.

ISBN: 979-8223872863

Written by Alex Thompson.

Also by Alex Thompson

Alex on Finance

Financial Freedom Roadmap - Achieving Early Retirement through the FIRE Movement
The Art of Strategic Innovation
Beyond Cash - The Evolution of Digital Payment Systems and the Future of Money
Preserving Wealth in Inflationary Times - Strategies for Protecting Your Financial Future

Standalone

Side Hustle Success: Unlocking Your Entrepreneurial Potential
Side Hustle Success: The Ultimate Guide to Passive and Financial Freedom
Mastering the Markets: Advanced Trading Strategies for Success and Ethical Trading Practices
Financial Fortitude
Mastering the Art of Upselling
The Financial Bullet Blueprint
Investing Demystified: A Beginner's Guide to Building Wealth in the Stock Market
Real Estate Riches: Building Wealth through Property Investment
How To Succeed as a Freelancer

Navigating Complex Waters: Advanced Strategies in Portfolio Management
Behavioral Finance and Investor Psychology
Leading with Empathy: Harnessing Emotional Intelligence for Effective Leadership
Financial Independence
Thriving Within Your Means: A Guide to Affordable Living
Algorithmic Trading: Navigating the Digital Frontier
Navigating Alternative Investments
Navigating the Behavioral Finance Landscape
Unlocking the Power of Derivatives
Mastering International Finance
Quantitative Finance and Risk Modeling
Sustainable and ESG Investing
Derivatives Dynamics: Navigating Risk and Innovation
Options Mastery: Navigating the Financial Frontier
Portfolio Mastery: Navigating the Financial Art and Science
Ethics in Hedge Funds: Navigating the Moral Compass of Finance
Structured Finance: Navigating Innovation, Sustainability and Ethics

Table of Contents

To all those who believe that the heart of finance beats not only with numbers but with ethics, integrity, and responsibility. Your commitment to a more ethical financial world inspires us all to reach higher, strive for transparency, and make a positive impact on the global financial landscape.

Chapter 1: Introduction to Hedge Funds

Definition and Characteristics of Hedge Funds

Hedge funds are a distinctive and enigmatic segment of the financial industry, characterized by a set of unique features that differentiate them from traditional investment vehicles.

1. Definition of Hedge Funds:

Hedge funds are private investment partnerships that aim to generate superior returns for their investors, known as limited partners, by employing a diverse range of investment strategies. Unlike traditional mutual funds, hedge funds operate with greater flexibility, both in terms of the asset classes they invest in and the strategies they employ. The term "hedge" in hedge funds originally referred to their objective of mitigating risk, but over time, hedge funds have evolved to encompass a broader spectrum of strategies, some of which are speculative and may involve higher levels of risk.

2. Characteristics of Hedge Funds:

◈ **Limited Partnership Structure:** Hedge funds typically operate as limited partnerships, where the fund manager or general partner manages the fund's assets, while investors are limited partners. Limited partners provide the capital, and the general partner manages it.

◈ **Investment Strategies:** Hedge funds employ a wide array of investment strategies, including long/short equity, global macro, event-driven, arbitrage, and quantitative strategies, among others. These strategies can be directional (betting on market movements) or non-directional (exploiting pricing discrepancies).

◈ **Lack of Regulation:** Hedge funds often operate with a degree of regulatory freedom compared to mutual funds. This flexibility allows them to pursue unconventional strategies and investment opportunities. However, it also means they are subject to fewer investor protection regulations.

◈ **Accredited Investors:** Hedge funds generally cater to accredited or sophisticated investors, who meet specific income or wealth criteria. This limitation is in place to ensure that investors have a certain level of financial sophistication and risk tolerance.

◈ **Performance Fees:** Unlike mutual funds, which typically charge management fees, hedge funds often charge both management fees and performance fees. Performance fees are a percentage of profits earned by the fund, aligning the interests of fund managers with those of investors.

◈ **Liquidity Terms:** Hedge funds often have restrictions on the liquidity of investments. Investors may be subject to lock-up periods during which they cannot redeem their investments, and redemption notices may have specific timeframes.

◈ **Use of Leverage:** Hedge funds commonly employ leverage to amplify returns. This involves borrowing funds to increase the size of their investments, potentially magnifying gains but also heightening risk.

◈ **Complex Investment Vehicles:** Hedge funds may invest in complex financial instruments, including derivatives, structured products, and illiquid assets. This complexity requires a deep understanding of financial markets and instruments.

◈ **Absolute Return Objective:** Hedge funds generally aim to achieve positive returns regardless of market conditions. This "absolute return" objective sets them apart from traditional funds, which may be benchmarked against market indices.

As we delve further into this book, we will explore each of these characteristics in greater detail and provide insights into the strategies, risks, and ethical considerations associated with hedge funds. Understanding these foundational elements is crucial for investors, fund managers, and anyone seeking to navigate the intricate world of hedge fund investments.

Historical Development of Hedge Funds

The history of hedge funds is a captivating journey through the evolution of investment management practices. To truly grasp the essence of hedge funds, it's essential to delve into their historical development, tracing their origins from the mid-20th century to the complex and diverse landscape we see today.

1. The Birth of Hedge Funds (1940s-1960s):

⟐ The concept of hedge funds originated in the United States during the late 1940s and early 1950s. Alfred Winslow Jones is widely regarded as the pioneer who created the first hedge fund, known as the "Hedged Fund," in 1949.

⟐ Jones's innovative idea was to use a combination of long and short positions to hedge against market risks, aiming to generate positive returns regardless of market conditions. This concept laid the foundation for what we now call "hedged" or "hedge" funds.

2. Growth and Expansion (1960s-1970s):

⟐ In the 1960s, hedge funds gained popularity among affluent investors and institutions due to their non-traditional strategies and potential for high returns.

◈ During this period, hedge fund managers began exploring various strategies, including merger arbitrage, event-driven investing, and global macro strategies. These strategies aimed to profit from corporate events, economic trends, and market anomalies.

3. Regulatory Changes and Industry Challenges (1980s-1990s):

◈ The 1980s saw regulatory changes that shaped the hedge fund industry. The Securities and Exchange Commission (SEC) introduced rules that allowed hedge funds to advertise and market themselves more openly.

◈ The 1990s brought both opportunities and challenges. Hedge funds grew in number and assets under management (AUM). However, the industry faced criticism and scrutiny due to high-profile collapses and scandals.

4. Modern Era (2000s-Present):

◈ The 21st century marked a period of significant growth and diversification in the hedge fund industry. New strategies, including quantitative and algorithmic trading, emerged.

◈ The global financial crisis of 2008 had a profound impact on the hedge fund industry. Many funds faced significant losses, and some were forced to shut down. It prompted investors to reconsider their allocations and risk management practices.

5. Regulatory Landscape (Post-Financial Crisis):

◈ In the aftermath of the financial crisis, regulatory scrutiny intensified. The Dodd-Frank Wall Street Reform and Consumer Protection Act in the United States introduced greater transparency and oversight for hedge funds.

◈ Globally, regulators introduced measures to enhance risk management and protect investors, particularly through improved reporting and transparency requirements.

6. The Rise of Quantitative and Systematic Strategies:

◈ The 21st century also witnessed the ascension of quantitative hedge funds, often referred to as "quants." These funds employ mathematical models and algorithms to make investment decisions, emphasizing data analysis and automation.

7. Ethical Considerations and Sustainable Investing:

◈ More recently, there has been a growing emphasis on ethical considerations and sustainability in the hedge fund industry. Some funds incorporate environmental, social, and governance (ESG) factors into their investment processes.

Understanding the historical development of hedge funds provides valuable context for evaluating their present state and future prospects. As we delve deeper into this book, we will explore the strategies, risk management practices, and ethical dimensions of hedge funds in the contemporary financial landscape. This historical journey underscores the enduring relevance and adaptability of hedge funds as financial instruments that continue to shape the world of investment.

Hedge Fund Strategies and Objectives

Hedge funds are a diverse group of investment vehicles, each employing distinct strategies and pursuing specific objectives. To navigate the complex landscape of hedge funds effectively, it's crucial to understand the various strategies they employ and the objectives they aim to achieve.

1. Investment Strategies:

◈ **Long/Short Equity:** Long/short equity hedge funds take both long (buy) and short (sell) positions in equities. They aim to generate returns by selecting undervalued stocks (long) and betting against overvalued stocks (short).

◈ **Event-Driven:** Event-driven hedge funds seek to profit from corporate events such as mergers and acquisitions, bankruptcies, spin-offs, and restructurings. These funds aim to capitalize on price inefficiencies created by these events.

◈ **Global Macro:** Global macro hedge funds make bets on broad macroeconomic trends and events, including currency movements, interest rates, and geopolitical developments. Their objective is to profit from macroeconomic shifts.

◈ **Arbitrage:** Arbitrage strategies involve exploiting price discrepancies between related assets or markets. For example, convertible arbitrage focuses on price differences between convertible bonds and their underlying stocks.

◈ **Quantitative/Algorithmic:** Quantitative hedge funds, often referred to as "quants," employ mathematical models and algorithms to make trading decisions. They aim to identify patterns and anomalies in financial markets.

2. Risk and Return Objectives:

◈ **Absolute Return:** Many hedge funds have an absolute return objective, meaning they aim to generate positive returns regardless of overall market performance. This sets them apart from traditional funds, which may be benchmarked against market indices.

◈ **Capital Preservation:** Some hedge funds prioritize capital preservation above all else. They aim to minimize the risk of significant losses and focus on preserving investor capital.

◈ **Risk-Adjusted Returns:** Hedge funds often emphasize achieving attractive risk-adjusted returns. This means they aim to generate returns that justify the level of risk taken, typically measured by metrics like the Sharpe ratio.

◈ **Alpha Generation:** Hedge funds aspire to generate alpha, which represents the portion of returns that cannot be attributed to market movements. Alpha is considered a measure of a fund manager's skill in selecting investments.

◈ **Leverage Utilization:** Certain hedge funds employ leverage to amplify returns. While this increases potential gains, it also heightens risk. Their objective may be to magnify returns within acceptable risk parameters.

3. Investor-Specific Objectives:

◈ **Diversification:** Hedge funds are often used as a diversification tool within an investor's portfolio. Investors seek to reduce portfolio risk by allocating to hedge funds with low correlations to traditional assets.

◈ **Income Generation:** Some hedge funds, particularly those specializing in credit strategies, aim to provide consistent income to investors through interest payments and dividends.

◈ **Tail Risk Hedging:** In times of heightened market uncertainty, hedge funds that focus on tail risk hedging aim to protect investors from extreme market events and minimize potential losses.

◈ **Long-Term Growth:** While hedge funds are known for their flexibility and focus on short- to medium-term opportunities, some investors allocate to them with a long-term growth objective.

Understanding these diverse hedge fund strategies and objectives is fundamental for investors, as it enables them to align their investment goals and risk tolerances with the appropriate hedge fund strategies. As we progress through this book, we will delve deeper into each strategy, exploring their nuances, risk management practices, and ethical considerations in greater detail. This comprehensive understanding will empower investors to make informed decisions in the dynamic world of hedge fund investing.

Role of Hedge Funds in the Financial Markets

Hedge funds play a multifaceted and dynamic role in the global financial markets. To gain a comprehensive understanding of these sophisticated investment vehicles, it is essential to explore their significance and influence in the broader financial landscape.

1. Liquidity Providers:

◈ Hedge funds often act as liquidity providers in the financial markets. Their active trading strategies, including arbitrage and market-making, contribute to market liquidity. This is particularly valuable during periods of market stress when liquidity can become scarce.

◈ Market liquidity is essential for the smooth functioning of financial markets, enabling investors to buy and sell assets with ease. Hedge funds, with their ability to quickly enter and exit positions, enhance market efficiency.

2. Price Discovery and Efficiency:

◈ Hedge funds engage in a wide range of strategies, from fundamental analysis to quantitative modeling. Their trading activities contribute to the price discovery process by incorporating new information and reflecting market sentiment.

◈ By participating in various markets and asset classes, hedge funds help ensure that asset prices accurately reflect supply and demand dynamics, contributing to market efficiency.

3. Risk Management:

◈ Hedge funds are skilled in employing strategies that mitigate risks. Their ability to take short positions, hedge against adverse market movements, and employ sophisticated risk management techniques can help stabilize financial markets.

◈ During periods of market turbulence, hedge funds often serve as a counterbalance to excessive market exuberance or panic, promoting stability.

4. Capital Allocation:

◈ Hedge funds allocate capital to a diverse array of investments, including equities, fixed income, derivatives, and alternative assets. This allocation of capital plays a crucial role in channeling funds to sectors and companies that offer growth potential.

◈ Their ability to engage in various investment strategies allows hedge funds to identify opportunities and allocate capital dynamically, contributing to economic growth.

5. Innovation and Strategy Development:

◈ Hedge funds are at the forefront of financial innovation. They pioneer new trading strategies, develop advanced risk management techniques, and drive the evolution of financial instruments and derivatives.

◈ Their innovative approach often leads to the creation of new investment opportunities and contributes to the evolution of financial markets.

6. Diverse Investment Options:

◈ Hedge funds offer investors a wide range of investment options and strategies, from long/short equity to event-driven and quantitative strategies. This diversity allows investors to tailor their portfolios to meet specific objectives and risk profiles.

◈ Investors can access unique investment opportunities that may not be available through traditional investment vehicles.

7. Performance Benchmarking:

◈ Hedge funds often serve as performance benchmarks for institutional investors and asset managers. Their returns, risk-adjusted performance, and correlation with traditional asset classes are used as reference points for evaluating investment strategies.

◈ Institutional investors and asset managers assess their own performance relative to hedge fund benchmarks, aiming to generate alpha and outperform these references.

8. Global Market Participation:

◈ Hedge funds operate in global financial markets, participating in both developed and emerging economies. Their international reach enables them to diversify portfolios across geographic regions, reducing risk.

◈ Their involvement in emerging markets can also contribute to the development and deepening of these markets.

In summary, hedge funds are dynamic participants in the financial markets, providing liquidity, contributing to price discovery, managing risks, allocating capital, fostering innovation, offering diverse investment options, and serving as performance benchmarks. Their role is integral to the functioning and evolution of the global financial system. As we progress through this book, we will delve deeper into the intricacies of hedge fund strategies, risk management practices, and ethical considerations, offering a comprehensive view of their impact on the financial world.

Regulatory Environment for Hedge Funds

Hedge funds, as complex and versatile financial entities, operate within a regulatory framework that aims to strike a balance between facilitating their activities and safeguarding the interests of investors and the stability of financial markets.

1. Securities and Exchange Commission (SEC):

◈ In the United States, the SEC plays a prominent role in regulating hedge funds. Hedge funds with more than $150 million in assets under management are required to register with the SEC under the Investment Advisers Act of 1940.

◈ Registered hedge funds must adhere to reporting requirements, providing disclosure documents to investors and the SEC. This enhances transparency and accountability.

◈ The SEC also conducts examinations and investigations to ensure compliance with securities laws and the prevention of fraudulent activities.

2. Dodd-Frank Wall Street Reform and Consumer Protection Act:

◈ Enacted in the aftermath of the 2008 financial crisis, Dodd-Frank introduced significant regulatory changes affecting hedge funds. It mandated registration and reporting for hedge funds with assets over a certain threshold.

◈ Dodd-Frank also created the Financial Stability Oversight Council (FSOC), which monitors and addresses systemic risks, including those posed by hedge funds.

3. Commodity Futures Trading Commission (CFTC):

◈ Hedge funds engaged in commodity trading or derivatives activities are subject to CFTC oversight. They may need to register as commodity pool operators (CPOs) or commodity trading advisors (CTAs).

◈ The CFTC enforces rules related to position limits, risk disclosures, and anti-fraud provisions for hedge funds operating in commodity markets.

4. Anti-Money Laundering (AML) and Know Your Customer (KYC) Regulations:

◈ Hedge funds are subject to AML and KYC regulations to prevent money laundering and terrorist financing. They must establish procedures for identifying and verifying the identity of clients and reporting suspicious transactions.

◈ These regulations help ensure that hedge funds are not unwittingly used for illicit activities.

5. International Regulatory Cooperation:

◈ Hedge funds often operate across borders, requiring cooperation between regulatory authorities in different countries. Initiatives like the Alternative Investment Fund Managers Directive (AIFMD) in Europe aim to harmonize regulations for hedge funds operating in the European Union.

◈ Global standards and agreements facilitate the exchange of information and the oversight of cross-border activities.

6. Investor Protections:

◈ Regulations governing hedge funds aim to protect investors by ensuring that they receive adequate disclosure, including information about risks, fees, and conflicts of interest.

◈ Regulations may also restrict the types of investors who can participate in hedge funds, often limiting access to accredited or institutional investors.

7. Risk Management and Reporting:

◈ Hedge funds are often required to implement robust risk management practices and reporting systems. This includes stress testing, liquidity risk management, and risk disclosures to investors.

◈ Reporting requirements may involve periodic updates on the fund's performance, holdings, and compliance with regulatory standards.

8. Ethical Considerations:

◈ Ethical standards and codes of conduct play a crucial role in the regulatory framework for hedge funds. Regulations often include provisions to prevent insider trading, market manipulation, and fraudulent activities.

◈ Ethical considerations also extend to issues like fair treatment of investors and conflicts of interest.

Navigating the regulatory environment is a fundamental aspect of hedge fund management. Compliance with these regulations is not only a legal obligation but also essential for maintaining trust with investors and ensuring the integrity of financial markets. As we progress through this book, we will explore the impact of regulations on hedge fund operations and delve deeper into the ethical considerations that guide their activities within this regulatory framework.

Chapter 2: Hedge Fund Strategies

Long/Short Equity Strategies

Long/short equity strategies are among the most well-known and widely employed by hedge funds. These strategies involve taking both long and short positions in equities, seeking to profit from both rising and falling stock prices.

1. Objectives of Long/Short Equity Strategies:

◈ **Alpha Generation:** Long/short equity managers aim to generate alpha, which represents returns in excess of a benchmark index or the broader market. This alpha can be achieved by selecting undervalued stocks for long positions and overvalued stocks for short positions.

◈ **Risk Mitigation:** These strategies also focus on mitigating market risk. By holding both long and short positions simultaneously, hedge funds aim to reduce exposure to overall market movements, making their returns less dependent on market direction.

2. Stock Selection and Fundamental Analysis:

◈ Successful long/short equity strategies rely heavily on in-depth fundamental analysis. Managers conduct rigorous research to identify companies with strong growth potential (long candidates) and companies with weaknesses or overvaluation (short candidates).

◈ Factors such as financial health, competitive position, industry trends, and management quality are evaluated for each stock in the portfolio.

3. Risk Management Techniques:

◈ **Pair Trading:** Long/short equity managers often pair long and short positions in similar or related companies. For example, they might go long on a stock in the automotive sector while simultaneously shorting a competitor in the same sector. This minimizes sector-specific risk.

◈ **Position Sizing:** Proper position sizing is crucial to manage risk. Hedge funds allocate capital to long and short positions based on their conviction levels and risk assessments. Risk limits and stop-loss orders are also commonly used.

4. Market Neutral vs. Directional Strategies:

◈ Long/short equity strategies can be market-neutral or directional. Market-neutral strategies aim to maintain a near-zero beta to the broader market, focusing solely on stock-specific factors. Directional strategies may have a higher beta and rely on market trends to some extent.

◈ Market-neutral strategies often involve equal dollar amounts of long and short positions to achieve a neutral market exposure.

5. Leverage and Financing:

◈ Hedge funds may use leverage to enhance returns. Leverage involves borrowing capital to increase the size of positions. However, it also amplifies risk, and careful risk management is essential when using leverage.

◈ Financing costs and margin requirements are considerations in the implementation of long/short equity strategies.

6. Liquidity and Short-Selling Considerations:

◈ Short selling involves borrowing shares of a stock and selling them in the hope of repurchasing them at a lower price. Hedge funds must consider the availability of borrowable shares and the potential for short squeezes when executing short positions.

◈ Liquidity is also important for both long and short positions. Illiquid stocks can be challenging to trade and may impact execution prices.

7. Performance and Benchmarking:

◈ Long/short equity funds are typically benchmarked against equity indices. Their performance is evaluated based on their ability to outperform these benchmarks while managing risk.

◈ Common benchmarks include the S&P 500 for U.S.-focused funds and regional or sector-specific indices for more specialized strategies.

8. Diversification:

◈ Diversification is a key risk management tool for long/short equity funds. By holding a diversified portfolio of long and short positions across various sectors and industries, they reduce the impact of individual stock-specific events.

◈ Over-concentration in a single stock or sector can lead to heightened risk.

Long/short equity strategies provide a versatile approach to equity investing, allowing hedge funds to profit in both bull and bear markets. Their success hinges on effective stock selection, risk management, and the ability to generate alpha.

Global Macro and Tactical Asset Allocation

Global macro and tactical asset allocation strategies represent a dynamic and macroeconomic-driven approach to hedge fund investing.

1. Objectives of Global Macro and Tactical Asset Allocation Strategies:

◈ **Macroeconomic Insights:** Hedge funds employing these strategies aim to capitalize on macroeconomic trends and global events. Their objective is to generate returns by correctly predicting and positioning for economic shifts.

◈ **Diversification:** Global macro funds often diversify across asset classes, including currencies, commodities, equities, and fixed income, seeking to spread risk and exploit opportunities across various markets.

2. Investment Tactics:

◈ **Top-Down Approach:** Managers of global macro and tactical asset allocation funds take a top-down approach to investing. They analyze macroeconomic indicators, geopolitical developments, and central bank policies to form their investment theses.

◈ **Dynamic Asset Allocation:** These strategies involve actively adjusting asset allocations based on changing economic conditions. For example, if a manager anticipates rising inflation, they may increase exposure to commodities or inflation-protected securities.

3. Risk Management Techniques:

◈ **Scenario Analysis:** Hedge funds using global macro strategies conduct scenario analysis to assess the potential impact of different economic scenarios on their portfolios. This helps them prepare for various outcomes.

◈ **Position Sizing:** Managers determine the size of their positions based on their conviction in a particular trade and their assessment of the associated risks.

4. Tactical vs. Strategic Allocations:

◈ Tactical asset allocation refers to short-term adjustments in response to changing market conditions or events. Strategic asset allocation, on the other hand, involves longer-term positioning based on fundamental economic views.

◈ Funds may incorporate a blend of both tactics, depending on their investment horizon and outlook.

5. Currency and Commodity Exposure:

◈ Global macro strategies often involve significant exposure to currencies and commodities. Managers may take speculative positions in currencies based on expected exchange rate movements or invest in commodities as a hedge against inflation or geopolitical risks.

◈ Currency and commodity markets can introduce additional volatility and risk.

6. Liquidity and Implementation:

◈ Liquidity management is crucial for these strategies, as they often involve trading across various asset classes. Hedge funds need to ensure that they can execute their positions without causing significant market disruptions.

◈ Implementation may involve using derivatives, such as futures and options, to gain exposure to specific markets or assets.

7. Performance and Benchmarking:

◈ Global macro and tactical asset allocation funds are typically benchmarked against a blend of indices that represent the various asset classes they invest in.

◈ Performance evaluation considers both returns and risk-adjusted metrics, such as the Sharpe ratio.

8. Geopolitical Analysis:

◈ Geopolitical events and developments play a significant role in these strategies. Managers closely follow geopolitical trends and assess their potential impact on financial markets and economies.

◈ Accurate geopolitical analysis is essential for making informed investment decisions.

9. Monitoring Economic Indicators:

◈ Managers continuously monitor a broad array of economic indicators, such as GDP growth, inflation rates, employment figures, and central bank policies. These indicators guide their investment decisions.

◈ Timely access to economic data and real-time news is critical for staying informed.

Global macro and tactical asset allocation strategies require a deep understanding of global economic dynamics and the ability to adapt to rapidly changing conditions. Hedge funds employing these strategies seek to identify investment opportunities arising from macroeconomic trends and geopolitical events.

Event-Driven and Merger Arbitrage Strategies

Event-driven and merger arbitrage strategies are a specialized subset of hedge fund strategies that focus on profiting from corporate events, such as mergers, acquisitions, restructurings, and other significant corporate actions.

1. Objectives of Event-Driven and Merger Arbitrage Strategies:

◈ **Capitalize on Corporate Events:** Hedge funds employing these strategies aim to profit from price inefficiencies created by corporate events. These events can include mergers, acquisitions, spin-offs, bankruptcies, and other corporate actions.

◈ **Risk Mitigation:** Event-driven strategies often aim to reduce market risk by focusing on specific events that may be less correlated with broader market movements. They seek to generate returns that are less dependent on market direction.

2. Investment Tactics:

◈ **Identifying Opportunities:** Managers conduct extensive research to identify potential event-driven opportunities. They analyze the terms of corporate events, assess the likelihood of successful outcomes, and estimate the potential returns.

◈ **Positioning for the Event:** Once an opportunity is identified, hedge funds take positions in the relevant securities. In the case of merger arbitrage, this often involves simultaneously buying shares of the target company and shorting shares of the acquiring company.

3. Risk Management Techniques:

◈ **Event Probability Analysis:** Managers assess the probability of the event's successful completion and adjust their positions accordingly. They may reduce exposure if the probability of the event falling through increases.

◈ **Diversification:** Event-driven strategies may involve holding a portfolio of event-driven positions to reduce the impact of individual event outcomes. Diversification can help mitigate risk.

4. Merger Arbitrage vs. Distressed Debt:

◈ While merger arbitrage focuses on profiting from the price differential between the target and acquiring companies during a merger or acquisition, distressed debt strategies involve investing in the debt of financially troubled companies with the expectation of a turnaround.

◈ Both strategies require in-depth analysis and a thorough understanding of the specific corporate event.

5. Special Situations:

◈ Special situations may include events such as spin-offs, rights offerings, and proxy contests. Hedge funds specializing in event-driven strategies assess the unique aspects of each situation to determine their investment approach.

6. Performance and Benchmarking:

◈ Event-driven and merger arbitrage funds are typically benchmarked against relevant indices that track the performance of companies involved in corporate events.

◈ Performance evaluation considers returns, risk-adjusted metrics, and the ability to capture event-related alpha.

7. Deal Timing and Execution:

◈ Timely execution is crucial in these strategies. Managers need to execute their trades before the market fully reflects the expected event outcomes, as prices can adjust rapidly once information becomes widely known.

◈ Deal completion timelines can vary, so patience and monitoring are key.

8. Legal and Regulatory Considerations:

⟐ Legal and regulatory factors play a significant role in these strategies. Managers must navigate securities laws, antitrust regulations, and other legal considerations when participating in corporate events.

⟐ Close collaboration with legal and compliance teams is essential.

9. Impact of Market Conditions:

⟐ Market conditions, such as interest rates and overall economic sentiment, can influence the success of event-driven strategies. Managers adapt their approach based on prevailing market conditions.

10. Realizing Profits:

⟐ Realizing profits in event-driven and merger arbitrage strategies often involves closing out positions once the event is completed. This can result in short holding periods compared to other hedge fund strategies.

Event-driven and merger arbitrage strategies require a keen understanding of corporate actions, deal structures, and legal nuances. Successful implementation hinges on thorough research, risk management, and timely execution.

Fixed Income and Credit Strategies

Fixed income and credit strategies encompass a broad range of hedge fund approaches focused on debt instruments and credit markets.

1. Objectives of Fixed Income and Credit Strategies:

⟐ **Generate Income:** Hedge funds employing these strategies aim to generate income by investing in a variety of fixed income securities, such as government bonds, corporate bonds, and credit derivatives.

◈ **Capital Preservation:** These strategies often prioritize capital preservation by investing in relatively low-risk debt instruments. However, some funds may incorporate higher-yield or distressed debt for greater returns.

2. Investment Tactics:

◈ **Asset Selection:** Managers of fixed income and credit hedge funds carefully select a mix of fixed income securities based on their credit quality, yield, duration, and other factors. They may invest in government bonds, investment-grade corporate bonds, high-yield bonds (junk bonds), municipal bonds, or credit default swaps.

◈ **Duration Management:** Managers actively manage the duration of their fixed income portfolios to mitigate interest rate risk. They adjust the average maturity of their holdings based on interest rate expectations.

3. Risk Management Techniques:

◈ **Credit Analysis:** A critical aspect of these strategies is conducting thorough credit analysis. Managers assess the creditworthiness of issuers to avoid defaults and credit events.

◈ **Diversification:** Diversification across different types of fixed income securities and issuers helps spread risk. It reduces the impact of any single default on the overall portfolio.

4. Yield vs. Risk:

◈ Hedge funds in this category must strike a balance between seeking higher yields, which often come with increased credit risk, and preserving capital.

◈ Some funds specialize in distressed debt, which involves investing in the debt of financially troubled companies in the hope of a successful turnaround.

5. Income Generation:

◈ Generating income is a primary goal, and funds may use strategies such as carry trades, interest rate swaps, and yield curve positioning to enhance returns.

6. Performance and Benchmarking:

◈ Fixed income and credit hedge funds are benchmarked against relevant fixed income indices, such as government bond or corporate bond indices.

◈ Performance evaluation considers returns, yield, credit quality, and risk-adjusted metrics.

7. Liquidity Management:

◈ Liquidity management is crucial in these strategies. Hedge funds must ensure they can meet redemption requests from investors while holding a portfolio of relatively illiquid fixed income securities.

◈ Liquidity risk is carefully managed to prevent forced selling at unfavorable prices.

8. Interest Rate Risk and Yield Curve Positioning:

◈ Funds actively monitor interest rate movements and may adjust portfolio duration to position for changes in interest rates.

◈ They may employ yield curve strategies, such as steepening or flattening the yield curve, to capture potential price movements.

9. Credit Events and Default Scenarios:

◈ Hedge funds specializing in credit strategies closely monitor credit events and potential defaults. They must be prepared to take action, such as selling or hedging positions, in response to deteriorating credit conditions.

10. Impact of Economic Factors:

◈ Economic factors, such as changes in inflation, economic growth, and central bank policies, can significantly impact fixed income and credit markets. Funds adjust their strategies accordingly.

Fixed income and credit strategies offer investors opportunities for income generation and capital preservation within the fixed income asset class. The success of these strategies relies on rigorous credit analysis, duration management, and the ability to adapt to evolving market conditions.

Systematic and Quantitative Strategies

Systematic and quantitative strategies represent a subset of hedge fund approaches characterized by their reliance on data-driven models, algorithms, and systematic trading rules.

1. Objectives of Systematic and Quantitative Strategies:

◈ **Alpha Generation:** Hedge funds employing systematic and quantitative strategies aim to generate alpha, or excess returns, by leveraging data-driven models and systematic trading approaches.

◈ **Risk Management:** These strategies often prioritize risk management through the use of quantitative models that help identify and control risk factors.

2. Investment Tactics:

⟐ **Quantitative Models:** Managers of systematic and quantitative hedge funds develop and implement quantitative models that guide their investment decisions. These models may use historical data, mathematical algorithms, and statistical techniques.

⟐ **Algorithmic Trading:** Many funds in this category rely on algorithmic trading systems to execute trades efficiently and systematically. These algorithms can analyze market conditions and execute trades at optimal prices.

3. Risk Management Techniques:

⟐ **Risk Models:** Hedge funds in this category typically use sophisticated risk models to monitor and manage portfolio risk. These models can assess exposure to various risk factors, such as market volatility and correlations.

⟐ **Diversification:** Diversification is a key risk management technique. Funds spread their investments across various assets, markets, and strategies to reduce the impact of adverse events.

4. Data Analysis and Quantitative Research:

⟐ Quantitative hedge funds place a strong emphasis on data analysis and quantitative research. They use historical data to develop, test, and refine their trading models.

⟐ Advanced statistical techniques and machine learning may be employed to extract predictive signals from data.

5. High-Frequency vs. Systematic Value Strategies:

⟐ Systematic strategies encompass a wide spectrum, from high-frequency trading that seeks to profit from short-term market inefficiencies to systematic value strategies that focus on long-term value-based investing.

6. Performance and Benchmarking:

◈ Systematic and quantitative hedge funds often benchmark their performance against specific market indices or custom indices that reflect the strategies they employ.

◈ Performance evaluation considers returns, risk-adjusted metrics, and the ability of the quantitative models to capture alpha.

7. Trading Infrastructure:

◈ Trading infrastructure is a critical component. Hedge funds in this category invest in cutting-edge technology to support their systematic and algorithmic trading activities.

◈ Low-latency connectivity to markets and high-performance computing are essential for timely execution.

8. Risk Factors and Model Adaptation:

◈ Managers constantly monitor the performance of their models and adjust them as market conditions evolve. This adaptability is essential to maintain effectiveness.

9. Behavioral Biases and Market Anomalies:

◈ Quantitative models aim to exploit market inefficiencies and anomalies. They are designed to minimize behavioral biases that can affect human decision-making.

10. Ethical Considerations and Data Privacy:

◈ The use of quantitative models and data analysis raises ethical considerations and data privacy concerns. Funds must adhere to regulatory and ethical standards when handling data.

Systematic and quantitative strategies represent a data-driven and algorithmic approach to hedge fund investing. Success in these strategies hinges on the development of robust quantitative models, risk management capabilities, and adaptability to changing market dynamics.

Chapter 3: Fund of Hedge Funds (FoHFs)

Overview of Fund of Hedge Funds

In this chapter, we will delve into the world of Fund of Hedge Funds (FoHFs), a unique investment vehicle that pools capital from investors to allocate across a diversified portfolio of hedge funds. FoHFs serve as a gateway for investors seeking access to the diverse strategies employed by hedge funds while benefiting from professional due diligence and risk management.

1. The Purpose of Fund of Hedge Funds:

◈ **Diversification:** FoHFs are designed to provide investors with a diversified exposure to various hedge fund strategies and managers, spreading risk across a range of assets and approaches.

◈ **Risk Management:** They aim to enhance risk management by conducting thorough due diligence on underlying hedge funds, monitoring their performance, and ensuring adherence to investment guidelines.

2. Investment Tactics:

◈ **Manager Selection:** FoHFs meticulously select a roster of hedge fund managers, each specializing in specific strategies. The selection process includes extensive research, interviews, and ongoing evaluation.

◈ **Portfolio Construction:** FoHFs build portfolios that align with the investment objectives of their clients. These portfolios may include a mix of equity-oriented, fixed income, and alternative strategies.

3. Due Diligence and Manager Monitoring:

◈ **Thorough Due Diligence:** FoHFs conduct in-depth due diligence on hedge fund managers. This includes assessing the manager's track record, investment process, risk management practices, and operational infrastructure.

◈ **Ongoing Monitoring:** FoHFs continuously monitor the performance and risk profiles of underlying hedge funds. They take action if a manager deviates from the agreed-upon strategy or if performance lags.

4. Customized Portfolios:

◈ FoHFs often tailor portfolios to meet the unique needs and risk tolerance of their clients. This customization can involve varying allocations to different strategies and managers.

5. Risk Management Techniques:

◈ **Asset Allocation:** FoHFs employ asset allocation strategies to manage risk. They may overweight or underweight specific strategies based on market conditions and risk assessments.

◈ **Risk Analysis:** Sophisticated risk analysis tools help FoHFs assess the potential risks in their portfolios, including market risk, liquidity risk, and manager-specific risks.

6. Performance and Benchmarking:

◈ FoHFs evaluate their performance based on a combination of returns and risk-adjusted metrics. Benchmarks often include hedge fund indices that align with their portfolio composition.

◈ Risk-adjusted performance metrics such as the Sharpe ratio and information ratio are commonly used.

7. Fee Structure:

◈ FoHFs typically charge fees for their services, which are in addition to the fees charged by the underlying hedge funds. The fee structure varies but often includes management fees and performance fees.

8. Accessibility and Professional Management:

◈ FoHFs provide investors with access to a broad range of hedge fund strategies that may otherwise be challenging to access individually.

◈ They offer professional management, making hedge fund investing more accessible to a wider range of investors.

9. Alignment of Interests:

◈ FoHFs often align their interests with those of their investors by co-investing alongside them in the underlying hedge funds.

10. Challenges and Criticisms:

◈ Critics argue that FoHFs may add an additional layer of fees, potentially eroding returns. Additionally, the selection of underperforming hedge funds can weigh down overall returns.

◈ Some investors prefer direct investments in hedge funds to maintain more control and avoid the additional fees associated with FoHFs.

Fund of Hedge Funds are a valuable tool for investors seeking diversified exposure to hedge fund strategies with professional management and risk oversight. Success in this space relies on rigorous due diligence, effective manager selection, and the ability to construct portfolios that align with investors' objectives. As we explore various hedge fund strategies in this book, we will continue to delve into the intricacies of FoHFs and their role within the hedge fund industry.

FoHF Investment Objectives

In this section, we will delve deeper into the investment objectives that drive Fund of Hedge Funds (FoHFs). These objectives serve as guiding principles for FoHF managers as they construct portfolios and make investment decisions on behalf of their clients.

1. Diversification and Risk Mitigation:

◈ One of the primary objectives of FoHFs is to achieve diversification across various hedge fund strategies. By spreading investments across different strategies and asset classes, FoHFs aim to reduce portfolio risk and enhance stability.

◈ FoHFs recognize that diversification can help mitigate the impact of poor performance from individual hedge funds, as different strategies may perform well under varying market conditions.

2. Alpha Generation:

◈ FoHFs seek to generate consistent alpha, or risk-adjusted returns, for their investors. They aim to identify and allocate to hedge fund managers who have a track record of outperforming their benchmarks and peers.

◈ Alpha generation is a key measure of success for FoHFs, as it reflects their ability to add value beyond what could be achieved through traditional investments.

3. Customized Solutions:

◈ FoHFs often have the objective of tailoring investment solutions to meet the unique needs of their clients. They consider factors such as risk tolerance, investment horizon, and liquidity requirements when constructing portfolios.

◈ Customization ensures that FoHFs align their investment strategies with the financial goals and preferences of their investors.

4. Manager Selection and Due Diligence:

◈ FoHFs are committed to thorough manager selection and due diligence. They aim to identify skilled hedge fund managers with strong risk management practices and operational integrity.

◈ Successful manager selection is a critical objective, as it forms the foundation of FoHF performance.

5. Risk Management and Preservation of Capital:

◈ Preserving capital and managing risk is a paramount objective for FoHFs. They employ risk management techniques to monitor and control portfolio risk, including exposure to market volatility and potential drawdowns.

◈ Risk management practices are geared toward protecting investors' capital while seeking attractive returns.

6. Access to Niche Strategies:

◈ FoHFs may seek to provide investors with access to specialized or niche hedge fund strategies that are not easily accessible to individual investors.

◈ The objective is to offer a diverse array of strategies that can enhance returns and reduce risk through low correlation.

7. Professional Expertise:

◈ FoHFs aim to leverage their professional expertise and experience in hedge fund investing to benefit their clients. They offer investors access to a team of experts who understand the complexities of hedge fund strategies.

◈ This expertise extends to manager selection, due diligence, risk assessment, and portfolio construction.

8. Transparency and Reporting:

◈ FoHFs often prioritize transparency and regular reporting to their clients. They aim to provide investors with a clear understanding of their investments, including performance, risk exposure, and underlying manager details.

◈ Transparency enhances investor confidence and helps clients make informed decisions.

9. Performance Evaluation:

◈ Evaluating and measuring performance against agreed-upon benchmarks is a core objective. FoHFs use various metrics, including risk-adjusted returns and peer group comparisons, to assess their performance.

◈ Performance evaluation ensures that FoHFs are delivering on their investment objectives and adding value to their clients.

10. Alignment of Interests:

◈ FoHFs strive to align their interests with those of their clients. They may co-invest alongside investors in the underlying hedge funds to demonstrate their commitment to the investment strategies.

◈ This alignment ensures that FoHFs are focused on delivering positive outcomes for their clients.

Understanding these investment objectives is crucial for both FoHF managers and investors. These objectives shape the strategies and actions taken by FoHFs as they navigate the complex landscape of hedge fund investing. As we continue our exploration of FoHFs in this book, we will delve into how these objectives are translated into practical investment decisions and portfolio construction.

Due Diligence and Selection of Hedge Funds

In the world of Fund of Hedge Funds (FoHFs), the due diligence and selection process for hedge funds is a critical and intricate undertaking. FoHF managers have the responsibility to identify, evaluate, and invest in a portfolio of hedge funds that align with their investment objectives and risk-return profile.

1. Comprehensive Manager Assessment:

◈ FoHF managers conduct comprehensive assessments of hedge fund managers' qualifications, experience, and track records. They evaluate the team's expertise, investment philosophy, and alignment with FoHF objectives.

◈ Due diligence often involves in-depth interviews and meetings with the hedge fund managers to gain insights into their investment strategies and risk management practices.

2. Performance Analysis:

◈ Performance analysis is a central element of due diligence. FoHF managers scrutinize historical performance data to assess a hedge fund's ability to generate alpha and deliver consistent returns.

◈ Performance analysis extends beyond returns and includes metrics like Sharpe ratio, drawdowns, and correlation with benchmarks.

3. Risk Assessment:

◈ Evaluating risk is paramount in the due diligence process. FoHFs analyze a hedge fund's risk management framework, including risk models, stress testing, and risk controls.

◈ Understanding how a hedge fund identifies, measures, and mitigates risks is crucial to assess its suitability for the FoHF portfolio.

4. Investment Strategy Alignment:

◈ FoHFs ensure that the selected hedge funds align with their investment strategy objectives. They assess whether the strategies employed by hedge funds complement each other and contribute to portfolio diversification.

◈ Investment strategy alignment is essential to achieve the FoHF's investment goals.

5. Operational Due Diligence:

◈ Operational due diligence focuses on the operational and infrastructure aspects of hedge funds. FoHF managers examine fund governance, compliance procedures, and operational efficiency.

◈ This diligence helps identify any potential operational risks that could impact the stability of the hedge fund.

6. Regulatory Compliance:

◈ FoHFs verify that hedge funds comply with regulatory requirements in the jurisdictions where they operate. Compliance with regulations is crucial to mitigate legal and regulatory risks.

◈ Understanding a hedge fund's regulatory standing is vital for FoHF managers to ensure their investments are in compliance with applicable laws.

7. Liquidity Assessment:

⟐ Liquidity considerations play a role in hedge fund selection. FoHFs evaluate the liquidity terms of the hedge funds to align with their own liquidity requirements and redemption policies.

⟐ FoHFs must strike a balance between liquidity needs and potential return opportunities.

8. Fee Structure and Alignment of Interests:

⟐ Examining the fee structure is an essential part of due diligence. FoHF managers assess the fee arrangement to ensure it is fair and aligned with investors' interests.

⟐ Fee transparency and fee-sharing agreements are scrutinized to avoid conflicts of interest.

9. Risk Management Practices:

⟐ Risk management practices within hedge funds are closely reviewed. FoHF managers assess how hedge funds identify and mitigate risks, including their risk monitoring and reporting processes.

⟐ An effective risk management framework enhances the stability of the hedge fund portfolio.

10. Ongoing Monitoring:

⟐ Due diligence is not a one-time process. FoHFs engage in ongoing monitoring of hedge fund investments to ensure that they continue to meet the required standards.

⟐ This monitoring includes performance tracking, risk assessment, and regular communication with hedge fund managers.

Effective due diligence and hedge fund selection are fundamental to the success of Fund of Hedge Funds. FoHF managers navigate a complex landscape, carefully curating a portfolio of hedge funds that collectively align with their investment objectives, risk appetite, and performance expectations.

FoHF Fee Structures

In the world of Fund of Hedge Funds (FoHFs), understanding fee structures is not only essential for the FoHF managers but also for the investors.

1. Management Fees:

◈ Management fees are the annual charges levied by FoHF managers for their services. These fees are typically calculated as a percentage of the FoHF's total assets under management (AUM).

◈ The management fee compensates FoHF managers for selecting and monitoring the hedge funds in the portfolio. It is a recurring cost that investors bear annually.

2. Performance Fees:

◈ Performance fees, also known as incentive fees, are tied to the returns generated by the FoHF above a specified hurdle rate. They are typically calculated as a percentage of the FoHF's profits.

◈ Performance fees incentivize FoHF managers to deliver alpha, as they only earn a fee when the portfolio outperforms the hurdle rate. This fee structure aligns the interests of FoHF managers with those of investors.

3. High-Water Mark:

◈ Many FoHFs employ a high-water mark mechanism when calculating performance fees. The high-water mark ensures that performance fees are only charged on new gains that surpass previous peaks in the portfolio's net asset value (NAV).

◈ This mechanism prevents FoHF managers from earning performance fees on the same gains repeatedly, enhancing fairness to investors.

4. Clawback Provisions:

◈ Clawback provisions are designed to rectify any overpaid performance fees. If, in subsequent years, the FoHF's performance falls below the high-water mark, the FoHF manager may be required to reimburse previously collected performance fees.

◈ Clawback provisions provide an additional layer of protection for investors by ensuring that FoHF managers only earn fees for sustained outperformance.

5. Fund Expenses:

◈ In addition to management and performance fees, FoHFs may incur expenses related to the operation of the fund. These expenses cover administrative, legal, and operational costs.

◈ Transparency regarding fund expenses is critical for investors to understand the total cost of investing in a FoHF.

6. Fee Negotiation:

◈ Fee structures within FoHFs are not set in stone. Investors often have the opportunity to negotiate fees with FoHF managers, especially when making significant investments.

◈ Negotiating fees can lead to more favorable terms for investors, potentially enhancing overall returns.

7. Impact on Investor Returns:

◈ The fee structure can significantly impact investor returns. High management and performance fees can erode returns, especially in periods of lower performance.

◈ Investors should carefully consider fee structures when evaluating the attractiveness of a FoHF investment.

8. Fee Transparency:

◈ Fee transparency is crucial for investor confidence. FoHF managers should provide clear and concise fee disclosures in fund documents.

◈ Investors have the right to understand how fees are structured and how they impact their investment.

9. Aligning Interests:

◈ Fee structures play a role in aligning the interests of FoHF managers with those of investors. Performance fees, in particular, encourage FoHF managers to strive for strong performance.

◈ An aligned fee structure helps ensure that FoHF managers are motivated to deliver value to investors.

10. Fee Reporting and Communication:

◈ FoHF managers should maintain open lines of communication with investors regarding fees. They should provide regular fee reports and updates on the fund's performance.

◈ Transparent communication helps investors stay informed about the cost of their investments.

Understanding the intricacies of fee structures in Fund of Hedge Funds is paramount for both FoHF managers and investors. Fee transparency, negotiation, and alignment of interests are key elements that contribute to a successful FoHF investment.

Chapter 4: Risk Management in Hedge Funds

Risk Factors in Hedge Fund Investments

Investing in hedge funds presents investors with a unique set of risk factors that require a comprehensive understanding and effective risk management strategies. This chapter explores the various risk factors associated with hedge fund investments, providing insights into the complexities and challenges investors face in this dynamic asset class.

Market Risk:

1. **Market Volatility:** Hedge funds are exposed to market volatility, which can result from economic events, geopolitical factors, or unexpected market shocks. Understanding and managing market risk is crucial for preserving capital.

2. **Systemic Risk:** Hedge funds can be affected by systemic risk, where market-wide disruptions impact multiple asset classes simultaneously. Systemic events can lead to significant losses if not properly managed.

Liquidity Risk:

3. **Redemption Risk:** Hedge funds often have lock-up periods or notice periods for redemptions. Investors may face liquidity constraints, especially during times of market stress.

4. **Underlying Asset Liquidity:** The liquidity of the underlying assets within hedge fund portfolios can vary widely. Illiquid assets may pose challenges during periods of high redemption requests.

Credit Risk:

5. **Counterparty Risk:** Hedge funds engage in various transactions involving counterparties. Counterparty risk arises when these counterparties fail to meet their financial obligations, potentially causing losses.

6. **Prime Broker Risk:** Hedge funds rely on prime brokers for services such as financing and execution. The financial stability of prime brokers is essential to hedge fund operations.

Operational Risk:

7. **Operational Failures:** Hedge funds are susceptible to operational failures, such as errors in trade execution, valuation discrepancies, or inadequate risk management procedures.

8. **Fraud and Misconduct:** Instances of fraud or misconduct within hedge funds can lead to substantial financial losses for investors.

Managerial Risk:

9. **Manager Skill and Strategy Risk:** The success of a hedge fund is highly dependent on the manager's skill and the efficacy of their investment strategy. Poor decision-making or strategy execution can result in underperformance.

10. **Key Person Risk:** In some cases, hedge funds rely heavily on the expertise and reputation of a key person. The departure or incapacitation of such individuals can affect fund performance.

Regulatory Risk:

11. **Regulatory Changes:** Changes in regulatory frameworks can impact hedge fund operations, compliance costs, and reporting requirements.

Risk Management Challenges:

12. **Lack of Transparency:** Hedge funds often provide limited transparency into their strategies and holdings, making it challenging for investors to assess and manage risks effectively.

13. **Complex Strategies:** Hedge funds employ a wide range of complex investment strategies that may be difficult for investors to fully comprehend, increasing the risk of unexpected outcomes.

Risk Mitigation Strategies:

14. **Diversification:** Diversifying investments across multiple hedge funds and strategies can help mitigate specific risk factors.

15. **Due Diligence:** Thorough due diligence on hedge fund managers, their strategies, and operational capabilities is essential to assess managerial risk and operational risk.

16. **Stress Testing:** Regular stress testing of portfolios can help identify vulnerabilities and assess the impact of adverse market scenarios.

17. **Risk Reporting:** Investors should have access to comprehensive risk reporting and portfolio analytics to monitor and manage risk effectively.

18. **Compliance and Regulation:** Staying informed about regulatory changes and ensuring compliance with reporting and disclosure requirements is crucial.

19. **Manager Selection:** Careful selection of hedge fund managers with a track record of risk management and transparency can enhance risk-adjusted returns.

Managing risk in hedge fund investments is a complex and ongoing process. It requires a combination of rigorous due diligence, effective diversification, and proactive risk management strategies. Investors should be aware of the specific risks associated with their chosen hedge funds and implement measures to mitigate these risks while aiming to achieve their investment objectives.

Measuring and Managing Market Risk in Hedge Funds

Market risk is a central concern for hedge fund investors and managers alike. In this section, we explore the intricacies of measuring and managing market risk within the context of hedge funds.

Market Risk Measurement:

1. **Value at Risk (VaR):** VaR is a widely used metric to estimate the potential loss in the value of a portfolio over a specific time horizon at a certain confidence level. Hedge funds calculate VaR to assess the downside risk of their positions and portfolios.

2. **Historical Simulation:** This method involves simulating portfolio returns based on historical market data. By analyzing past market movements, hedge funds can gain insights into how their portfolios may perform in various market conditions.

3. **Monte Carlo Simulation:** Monte Carlo simulations use random sampling to model potential future market scenarios. Hedge funds can employ this method to assess the impact of different market conditions on their portfolios.

4. **Sensitivity Analysis:** Hedge funds analyze how changes in key market variables, such as interest rates, exchange rates, and volatility, affect their portfolio values. This helps in understanding the sensitivity of the portfolio to various market factors.

Managing Market Risk:

5. **Asset Allocation:** Hedge funds can manage market risk through strategic asset allocation. By diversifying across different asset classes

and investment strategies, they can reduce exposure to specific market movements.

6. **Hedging Strategies:** Hedge funds often use derivative instruments such as futures and options to hedge against adverse market movements. For example, a long/short equity fund may use index futures to hedge against broad market declines.

7. **Dynamic Asset Allocation:** Some hedge funds employ dynamic asset allocation, adjusting their portfolio exposure based on changing market conditions. This flexibility allows them to reduce risk during periods of market uncertainty.

8. **Stress Testing:** Stress testing involves subjecting the portfolio to extreme market scenarios to assess potential losses. Hedge funds can use stress tests to identify vulnerabilities and adjust their risk management strategies accordingly.

9. **Stop-Loss Orders:** Hedge funds may implement stop-loss orders to limit losses on specific positions. When an asset's price reaches a predetermined level, the position is automatically sold to mitigate further losses.

10. **Scenario Analysis:** In addition to stress testing, scenario analysis involves simulating various market scenarios to understand how different conditions may impact the portfolio. Hedge funds can use this analysis for risk assessment and decision-making.

11. **Liquidity Management:** Ensuring sufficient liquidity is vital for managing market risk. Hedge funds must have access to cash or liquid assets to meet redemption requests or take advantage of investment opportunities during market downturns.

12. **Risk Reporting and Monitoring:** Regularly monitoring and reporting on market risk exposure is essential. Hedge funds should have

robust risk management systems in place to provide timely insights into portfolio risk.

13. **Regulatory Compliance:** Hedge funds must comply with regulatory requirements related to risk management and reporting. Staying abreast of regulatory changes and ensuring compliance is critical.

14. **Investor Communication:** Transparent communication with investors regarding market risk and risk management strategies builds trust and helps manage expectations.

15. **Continuous Learning:** The financial markets are dynamic, and new risks emerge over time. Hedge funds should prioritize ongoing education and adaptation to evolving market conditions.

Managing market risk in hedge funds requires a multifaceted approach that integrates quantitative modeling, risk assessment, and proactive risk mitigation strategies. Hedge fund managers must strike a balance between achieving investment objectives and safeguarding capital in the face of market uncertainties.

Managing Credit Risk and Counterparty Risk in Hedge Funds

Credit risk and counterparty risk are critical considerations for hedge funds, as they can significantly impact the fund's performance and stability. In this section, we explore how hedge funds manage these risks.

Credit Risk Management:

1. **Credit Analysis:** Hedge funds conduct thorough credit analysis of the securities they hold. This analysis assesses the creditworthiness of issuers, helping funds avoid investments in securities with a high likelihood of default.

2. **Diversification:** Diversifying across different issuers and asset classes can reduce credit risk. By holding a variety of assets, hedge funds can mitigate the impact of a single issuer's default.

3. **Credit Ratings:** Hedge funds often rely on credit ratings provided by rating agencies to assess the credit risk of securities. However, they also conduct their own analysis to supplement these ratings.

4. **Credit Derivatives:** Hedge funds use credit derivatives like credit default swaps (CDS) to hedge against credit risk. CDS can provide protection in case of issuer default, allowing funds to transfer the risk to other parties.

5. **Collateralization:** When entering into transactions involving credit risk, hedge funds may require counterparties to provide collateral. Collateral serves as a security measure to mitigate potential losses in the event of a default.

Counterparty Risk Management:

6. **Counterparty Due Diligence:** Hedge funds perform due diligence on their counterparties to assess their financial stability and creditworthiness. This includes evaluating their balance sheets, credit ratings, and reputation.

7. **Master Agreements:** Hedge funds use master agreements, such as the International Swaps and Derivatives Association (ISDA) agreement, to establish legal terms and conditions for transactions. These agreements specify how disputes and defaults are handled.

8. **Netting Arrangements:** Netting agreements allow hedge funds to offset obligations with a counterparty. This means that if one party owes money to the other, the net amount is settled, reducing exposure.

9. **Collateral Agreements:** Hedge funds may require counterparties to post collateral, which can be in the form of cash or securities. This collateral serves as a buffer against counterparty default.

10. **Monitoring Counterparty Risk:** Hedge funds continuously monitor the creditworthiness of their counterparties. If a counterparty's financial health deteriorates, the fund may take proactive measures to reduce exposure.

11. **Regulatory Compliance:** Hedge funds must comply with regulatory requirements related to counterparty risk management. These regulations often dictate capital adequacy standards and risk exposure limits.

12. **Stress Testing:** Stress testing involves assessing the impact of adverse scenarios, including counterparty defaults, on the fund's portfolio. Hedge funds use stress tests to evaluate the resilience of their strategies.

13. **Contingency Planning:** Hedge funds develop contingency plans to address counterparty defaults. These plans include identifying alternative counterparties and exit strategies.

14. **Counterparty Communication:** Open communication with counterparties is essential. Hedge funds should discuss risk management measures and ensure alignment on the terms of transactions.

15. **Operational Risk Mitigation:** Reducing operational risk, such as errors in trade processing or settlements, can indirectly mitigate counterparty risk. Hedge funds implement robust operational processes to minimize such risks.

Effective credit risk and counterparty risk management are integral to a hedge fund's ability to preserve capital and generate returns. By employing a combination of rigorous analysis, risk mitigation strategies, and regulatory compliance, hedge funds aim to navigate the complexities of credit and counterparty risk while pursuing their investment objectives.

Managing Liquidity Risk and Redemption Risk in Hedge Funds

Liquidity risk and redemption risk are significant concerns for hedge funds, as they can affect a fund's ability to meet investor redemptions and maintain portfolio stability.

Liquidity Risk Management:

1. **Asset Liquidity Assessment:** Hedge funds carefully assess the liquidity of the assets they hold. This involves evaluating the ease with which assets can be converted into cash without significantly affecting market prices.

2. **Liquidity Stress Testing:** Stress testing involves simulating scenarios where liquidity dries up or market conditions deteriorate. Hedge funds use stress tests to assess their portfolio's resilience in adverse liquidity conditions.

3. **Cash Management:** Hedge funds maintain sufficient cash and cash equivalents to meet short-term redemption requests without the need for fire sales of illiquid assets.

4. **Liquidity Buckets:** Funds may categorize their assets into different liquidity buckets, ranging from highly liquid to illiquid. This helps in managing the overall liquidity profile of the portfolio.

5. **Use of Lines of Credit:** Some hedge funds establish lines of credit with banks or financial institutions. These credit lines can be drawn upon in times of liquidity need, providing a buffer against redemptions.

6. **Gate Provisions:** Hedge funds may implement gate provisions in their offering documents, allowing them to limit or temporarily suspend redemptions during periods of extreme market stress. This helps protect the interests of remaining investors.

Redemption Risk Management:

7. **Notice Periods:** Hedge funds typically impose notice periods for redemptions, ranging from one to three months. This gives fund managers time to liquidate assets in an orderly manner to meet redemption requests.

8. **Lock-Up Periods:** Some hedge funds impose lock-up periods during which investors cannot redeem their investments. Lock-up periods can help fund managers maintain stability and implement their strategies effectively.

9. **Redemption Fees:** Hedge funds may charge redemption fees, also known as exit fees or gates, to discourage short-term investors from redeeming. These fees are typically a percentage of the redemption amount.

10. **High-Water Mark:** Hedge funds often use a high-water mark mechanism. This means that an investor can only redeem profits that exceed the highest historical net asset value (NAV) of their investment. This encourages long-term commitment.

11. **Side Pockets:** In cases where a hedge fund holds illiquid or hard-to-value assets, they may create side pockets. These side pockets segregate illiquid assets from the main portfolio, allowing fund managers to manage their disposition over time.

12. **Investor Communication:** Effective communication with investors is crucial. Hedge funds regularly update investors on the

fund's performance, liquidity conditions, and any relevant changes to redemption terms.

13. **Alignment of Interests:** Hedge funds strive to align the interests of fund managers and investors. This often involves portfolio managers having a significant portion of their wealth invested in the fund.

14. **Regulatory Compliance:** Hedge funds must comply with regulatory requirements related to liquidity management and redemption terms. These regulations often dictate notice periods and fee structures.

15. **Contingency Planning:** Hedge funds develop contingency plans for scenarios where redemption requests exceed available liquidity. This may involve negotiating with investors or implementing gates.

16. **Investor Education:** Educating investors about the fund's redemption terms, liquidity profile, and risk factors is essential. Informed investors are more likely to make rational decisions during times of stress.

Liquidity risk and redemption risk are inherent in hedge fund investing. Hedge funds employ a combination of strategies, including asset selection, portfolio construction, and risk management techniques, to mitigate these risks. Effective liquidity and redemption risk management contribute to the overall stability and success of hedge funds, allowing them to fulfill their investment objectives while providing liquidity to investors.

Managing Operational Risk and Preventing Fraud in Hedge Funds

Operational risk and fraud prevention are critical aspects of hedge fund management. Operational risk encompasses various factors that can disrupt fund operations, while fraud poses a threat to the integrity of the fund.

Operational Risk Management:

1. **Comprehensive Due Diligence:** Hedge funds conduct extensive due diligence when selecting service providers, including administrators, prime brokers, and custodians. This helps ensure that these entities have robust operational processes.

2. **Business Continuity Planning:** Hedge funds develop and regularly test business continuity plans to address potential disruptions, such as natural disasters, cyberattacks, or system failures. These plans outline procedures for maintaining essential operations during crises.

3. **Operational Controls:** Implementing robust operational controls and processes helps minimize the risk of errors and inefficiencies. Hedge funds employ experienced operations professionals to oversee these functions.

4. **Cybersecurity Measures:** In the digital age, cybersecurity is a top priority. Funds invest in advanced cybersecurity tools and protocols to safeguard sensitive data and protect against cyber threats.

5. **Employee Training:** Hedge fund employees receive training on operational risk management, including cybersecurity best practices, compliance procedures, and the identification of potential operational risks.

6. **Third-Party Oversight:** Funds monitor and assess the operational risk of third-party service providers, holding them to high standards of security, compliance, and risk management.

7. **Regulatory Compliance:** Hedge funds adhere to regulatory requirements related to operational risk management and reporting. This includes documenting operational incidents and implementing corrective actions.

Fraud Prevention:

8. **Internal Controls:** Hedge funds establish internal controls that segregate duties and create checks and balances within the organization. This reduces the risk of internal fraud.

9. **Code of Ethics:** Hedge funds adopt and enforce a comprehensive code of ethics that outlines expected behaviors and ethical standards for all employees. Violations are subject to disciplinary actions.

10. **Whistleblower Programs:** Whistleblower programs encourage employees to report unethical or fraudulent behavior anonymously. These programs provide protection to those who come forward.

11. **External Audits:** Regular external audits conducted by reputable audit firms help detect irregularities and fraud. Auditors examine financial records and internal controls to ensure compliance.

12. **Independent Valuation:** Hedge funds often employ independent valuation agents to value illiquid assets and ensure that pricing is not manipulated.

13. **Investor Transparency:** Hedge funds provide transparency to investors regarding their investments, including portfolio holdings, performance, and valuation methods. This transparency allows investors to monitor their investments for signs of fraud.

14. **Regulatory Compliance:** Hedge funds adhere to regulatory requirements related to fraud prevention and reporting. Compliance with regulations helps deter fraudulent activities.

15. **Background Checks:** Comprehensive background checks are conducted on potential employees and key personnel to identify any prior involvement in fraudulent activities.

16. **Conflict of Interest Policies:** Hedge funds establish and enforce conflict of interest policies to prevent personal interests from conflicting with the fund's interests.

17. **Independent Directors:** Some hedge funds appoint independent directors to the fund's board to provide an objective perspective and oversee fund operations, including fraud prevention.

18. **Fraud Investigations:** If fraud is suspected or detected, hedge funds initiate thorough investigations, involving legal and forensic experts, to gather evidence and take appropriate action.

Operational risk and fraud prevention are ongoing efforts in the hedge fund industry. Hedge funds dedicate substantial resources to these areas to protect the interests of their investors and maintain the integrity of their operations. By implementing robust operational practices, adhering to regulations, and fostering a culture of ethical behavior, hedge funds can reduce the likelihood and impact of operational disruptions and fraud.

Chapter 5: Performance Measurement and Attribution

Performance Metrics and Attribution in Hedge Funds

Performance measurement and attribution are essential aspects of hedge fund management. They allow investors, fund managers, and other stakeholders to evaluate the fund's performance, understand its sources of returns, and assess the effectiveness of investment strategies.

Hedge Fund Performance Metrics:

1. **Sharpe Ratio:** The Sharpe Ratio assesses a hedge fund's risk-adjusted return by comparing its excess return (return above the risk-free rate) to its volatility (standard deviation of returns). A higher Sharpe Ratio indicates better risk-adjusted performance.

2. **Sortino Ratio:** Similar to the Sharpe Ratio, the Sortino Ratio measures risk-adjusted returns but focuses solely on downside risk, considering only returns below a specified target or hurdle rate. It provides insight into a fund's ability to protect against losses.

3. **Alpha:** Alpha represents the excess return generated by a hedge fund beyond what would be expected based on its risk exposure. A positive alpha indicates that the fund has outperformed its benchmark or risk-adjusted expectations.

4. **Beta:** Beta measures a hedge fund's sensitivity to market movements. A beta of 1 implies the fund's returns move in line with the market, while a beta less than 1 suggests lower volatility, and a beta greater than 1 implies higher volatility.

5. **Information Ratio:** The Information Ratio evaluates a hedge fund's ability to generate excess returns relative to its benchmark. It quantifies the fund manager's skill in selecting investments and managing risk.

6. **Calmar Ratio:** The Calmar Ratio assesses a hedge fund's risk-adjusted performance by comparing the average annualized return to the maximum drawdown (the largest peak-to-trough decline). A higher Calmar Ratio indicates better risk-adjusted returns.

7. **Capture Ratios:** Capture ratios measure a hedge fund's ability to capture the upside and downside moves of a particular market or benchmark. These ratios are expressed as percentages and provide insight into the fund's directional exposure.

Performance Attribution:

8. **Asset Allocation Attribution:** This technique dissects a hedge fund's returns to determine how much can be attributed to asset allocation decisions. It helps evaluate the effectiveness of the fund's investment strategy.

9. **Security Selection Attribution:** Security selection attribution isolates the impact of individual investment decisions on a fund's returns. It quantifies the contribution of specific securities to the fund's overall performance.

10. **Factor Attribution:** Factor attribution analyzes the impact of systematic factors (such as interest rates, economic indicators, or market volatility) on a hedge fund's returns. It identifies which factors are driving performance.

11. **Interaction Effects Attribution:** Interaction effects attribution examines how multiple factors and investment decisions interact to influence a fund's returns. It provides a more nuanced understanding of performance drivers.

12. **Risk Attribution:** Risk attribution evaluates the contribution of risk factors to a hedge fund's returns. It helps identify which risks, such as credit risk or interest rate risk, had the most significant impact on performance.

13. **Benchmark Attribution:** Benchmark attribution compares a hedge fund's returns to a specified benchmark, such as an index or peer group. It assesses whether the fund outperformed or underperformed its chosen benchmark.

Performance Measurement Challenges:

14. **Illiquidity Adjustments:** Hedge funds often invest in illiquid assets, making performance measurement challenging. Adjustments may be required to account for the illiquidity premium or potential valuation discrepancies.

15. **Survivorship Bias:** Survivorship bias occurs when only successful hedge funds are included in performance databases, leading to an overestimation of average returns. Properly accounting for funds that have closed or failed is essential.

16. **Backfill Bias:** Backfill bias occurs when hedge funds add historical performance data to databases when they join, potentially inflating their historical returns. Analysts must account for this bias in performance analysis.

17. **Non-Normality of Returns:** Hedge fund returns often exhibit non-normal distributions, with fat tails and skewness. This makes standard performance metrics less informative, and alternative methods may be required.

Incorporating these performance metrics and attribution techniques allows hedge fund stakeholders to make informed investment decisions, assess risk-adjusted returns, and gain insights into the drivers of fund performance. Additionally, understanding the challenges associated with performance measurement is crucial for accurate evaluation and comparison of hedge funds.

Benchmarking Hedge Fund Returns:

Benchmarking hedge fund returns is a critical aspect of performance evaluation. It involves comparing a hedge fund's performance to a relevant benchmark or peer group to assess its relative success.

Importance of Benchmarking:

1. **Performance Assessment:** Benchmarking provides a basis for evaluating a hedge fund's performance. It allows investors to gauge whether the fund is meeting their expectations and objectives.

2. **Risk Evaluation:** By comparing a hedge fund's returns to a benchmark, investors can assess how much risk the fund is taking to achieve its performance. This is crucial for understanding the fund's risk-return profile.

3. **Manager Skill:** Benchmarking helps distinguish between skilled fund managers and those who may be benefiting from broader market trends. A hedge fund outperforming its benchmark is an indicator of manager skill.

4. **Investment Decision-Making:** Investors often use benchmarks to make investment decisions. If a hedge fund consistently underperforms its benchmark, investors may consider reallocating their capital elsewhere.

Challenges in Benchmarking Hedge Fund Returns:

Benchmarking hedge funds presents unique challenges due to their diverse strategies and objectives. Here are some of the challenges:

5. **Lack of Appropriate Benchmarks:** Hedge funds employ various strategies, and finding a single benchmark that accurately represents their performance can be challenging. Some hedge funds may require custom benchmarks.

6. **Benchmark Applicability:** A benchmark should be relevant to the hedge fund's strategy. For example, comparing a long/short equity fund to an equity index makes sense, but using the same benchmark for a fixed income arbitrage fund may not.

7. **Benchmark Selection Bias:** Hedge funds sometimes choose benchmarks that favor their performance. Investors need to be cautious about funds that cherry-pick benchmarks to appear more successful.

8. **Benchmark Timeframe:** The choice of the benchmark's timeframe can significantly impact the assessment of a hedge fund's performance. Short-term benchmarks may not accurately reflect long-term strategies.

Methodologies in Benchmarking:

9. **Peer Group Comparisons:** One common benchmarking method involves comparing a hedge fund's returns to those of its peers with similar strategies. Peer group comparisons provide a relative performance context.

10. **Index Benchmarks:** Hedge fund indices, such as the HFRI (Hedge Fund Research Index) or HFRX (Hedge Fund Research Index Fund of Funds Composite), are designed to represent the average performance of hedge funds within certain categories.

11. **Custom Benchmarks:** Some hedge funds, especially those with unique strategies, opt for custom benchmarks tailored to their specific objectives and risk profiles. These benchmarks are often constructed using a blend of market indices.

12. **Risk-Adjusted Benchmarks:** To account for risk, investors may use risk-adjusted benchmarks like the Modified Dietz method, which considers the fund's cash flows and the timing of returns.

Limitations of Benchmarking:

13. **Differences in Risk Profiles:** Hedge funds vary in their risk exposure and objectives. Benchmarking may not capture the full spectrum of risks taken by a fund, especially when comparing it to a single benchmark.

14. **Survivorship Bias:** Benchmarking databases may exclude underperforming or failed hedge funds, leading to survivorship bias. This can result in an overestimation of average hedge fund returns.

15. **Changing Benchmark Goals:** Over time, a hedge fund's strategy or objectives may evolve. This can make historical benchmark comparisons less relevant.

16. **Backfill and Look-Ahead Bias:** Hedge funds often include historical data in benchmark comparisons when they join a database. This can lead to backfill bias. Additionally, funds may engage in look-ahead bias by selecting benchmarks after observing their performance.

In summary, benchmarking is a valuable tool for evaluating hedge fund performance, but it comes with challenges that require careful consideration. Investors should choose benchmarks that align with a hedge fund's strategy, use risk-adjusted measures when possible, and be mindful of biases that can affect the accuracy of comparisons. Effective benchmarking enhances decision-making and helps investors allocate their capital wisely in the complex world of hedge funds.

Performance Attribution Analysis:

Performance attribution analysis is a powerful tool used by investors and portfolio managers to dissect and understand the sources of a portfolio's returns. This technique breaks down the overall return of a portfolio into various components, each of which represents a different driver of performance. Here, we explore the importance of performance attribution, its methodologies, and its role in investment decision-making.

Importance of Performance Attribution:

1. **Identifying Sources of Returns:** Performance attribution helps investors understand what factors contributed to a portfolio's overall return. This knowledge is crucial for making informed investment decisions.

2. **Performance Evaluation:** It allows investors to assess the skill of portfolio managers. By comparing actual returns to expected returns based on various factors, it becomes clear whether a manager's decisions added value or detracted from it.

3. **Risk Assessment:** Attribution analysis provides insights into the risks associated with different investment decisions. By attributing performance to specific factors, investors can gauge the risk exposures in their portfolios.

4. **Asset Allocation Optimization:** It assists investors in optimizing asset allocation. By identifying which asset classes or investment strategies are driving performance, investors can adjust their allocations accordingly.

Methodologies in Performance Attribution:

5. **Factor Attribution:** Factor-based attribution breaks down returns into factors such as asset allocation, security selection, and market

timing. It quantifies how each factor contributed to the portfolio's performance.

6. **Security-Level Attribution:** This method attributes returns to individual securities or holdings within the portfolio. It provides insights into the contribution of specific investments to overall performance.

7. **Sector and Industry Attribution:** For equity portfolios, this approach dissects returns by sectors or industries. It helps investors understand which sectors drove performance and which lagged.

8. **Attribution by Region or Geography:** In global portfolios, attributing performance by region or geography helps investors assess the impact of regional economic trends and geopolitical factors.

Components of Performance Attribution:

9. **Asset Allocation Effect:** This component measures the contribution of asset allocation decisions to portfolio performance. It assesses whether being overweight or underweight certain asset classes was beneficial.

10. **Security Selection Effect:** Security selection effect quantifies the impact of selecting individual securities within a given asset class or sector. It distinguishes between outperforming and underperforming securities.

11. **Interaction Effect:** Interaction effect, also known as the interaction of asset allocation and security selection, evaluates how the combined effect of allocation decisions and security selection impacted performance.

Limitations of Performance Attribution:

12. **Assumption Sensitivity:** Attribution analysis relies on certain assumptions about how returns are attributed to factors. Small changes in these assumptions can lead to different results.

13. **Overlapping Factors:** In complex portfolios, it can be challenging to isolate the impact of a single factor because factors often overlap. For example, a security may be influenced by both its sector and individual attributes.

14. **Data Quality:** Attribution analysis requires accurate and timely data, which may not always be available, particularly for less liquid or esoteric investments.

15. **Short-Term vs. Long-Term:** Attribution analysis is often more informative for longer time horizons. Short-term results may be dominated by noise and less meaningful.

Application of Performance Attribution:

16. **Portfolio Rebalancing:** Investors use attribution results to decide whether to rebalance their portfolios to capture specific sources of returns or reduce risks.

17. **Manager Evaluation:** Institutional investors and asset allocators employ attribution to evaluate the performance of external portfolio managers.

18. **Risk Management:** Attribution analysis helps identify risk exposures and provides insights into risk-adjusted performance.

19. **Performance Benchmarking:** Comparing a portfolio's attribution results to benchmarks helps investors understand how well their investments are aligned with their objectives.

20. **Communication with Clients:** Financial advisors and wealth managers use attribution analysis to explain portfolio performance to clients in a transparent and understandable manner.

Survivorship Bias and Backfill Bias in Hedge Fund Data Analysis:

Survivorship bias and backfill bias are two critical issues that can significantly impact the accuracy and reliability of hedge fund data analysis. Understanding these biases is essential for investors, researchers, and analysts to make informed decisions and avoid misinterpretation of hedge fund performance.

Survivorship Bias:

Survivorship bias occurs when unsuccessful hedge funds are excluded from the dataset, leading to an overestimation of hedge fund returns and a distorted view of the industry's overall performance. Here's an in-depth look at survivorship bias:

1. **Exclusion of Failed Funds:** Survivorship bias arises because failed or closed hedge funds are often removed from the dataset. As a result, only surviving funds with relatively better performance continue to be analyzed.

2. **Overestimation of Returns:** When underperforming funds are excluded, the reported average returns of hedge funds can be significantly higher than the true industry-wide average. This can create unrealistic expectations for potential investors.

3. **Misleading Performance Analysis:** Researchers and investors may base their decisions on a dataset that paints a more favorable picture of hedge fund performance than what is representative of the broader industry.

4. **Risk Assessment:** Survivorship bias can lead to an underestimation of the risks associated with hedge fund investments, as riskier or poorly performing funds are often the ones that cease operations.

Addressing Survivorship Bias:

To mitigate the impact of survivorship bias, analysts and investors should:

◈ **Use Survivorship-Bias-Corrected Data:** Whenever possible, use datasets that account for the performance of both surviving and failed funds. These corrected datasets provide a more accurate representation of hedge fund performance.

◈ **Understand Data Sources:** Be aware of the data sources used and inquire whether survivorship bias has been accounted for. Reliable data providers often offer survivorship-bias-adjusted datasets.

◈ **Consider All Available Information:** When analyzing hedge fund performance, consider qualitative factors, such as strategy, management team, and risk management, in addition to quantitative returns data.

Backfill Bias:

Backfill bias occurs when hedge funds selectively report historical performance data to databases, including only their best-performing periods. This bias can lead to an inaccurate assessment of a fund's true historical performance. Here's a closer look at backfill bias:

1. **Cherry-Picked Data:** Hedge funds may choose to "backfill" databases with historical returns only when they have performed well. This cherry-picking of data creates an upward bias in reported returns.

2. **Exaggeration of Skill:** Backfill bias can make a hedge fund appear more skilled or successful than it actually is, as it selectively highlights

favorable performance periods while omitting underperforming periods.

3. **Misleading Track Records:** Investors relying on historical performance data to assess a fund's track record may make decisions based on incomplete or skewed information.

Addressing Backfill Bias:

To address backfill bias, investors and analysts should:

⟐ **Be Cautious with Historical Data:** Exercise caution when relying on historical data, especially if it has been selectively provided by the hedge fund. Seek more complete and transparent performance records.

⟐ **Use Longer Time Horizons:** Consider longer-term performance records to gain a more comprehensive view of a fund's historical performance, rather than relying solely on recent returns.

⟐ **Verify Data Accuracy:** Cross-reference performance data from multiple sources and verify its accuracy to ensure it aligns with the fund's actual track record.

Evaluating and Selecting Hedge Funds:

Evaluating and selecting hedge funds is a crucial process for investors seeking to allocate capital to alternative investments. Hedge funds offer diverse strategies, risk profiles, and performance histories, making a comprehensive evaluation framework essential. Here's an in-depth guide to help investors navigate this process:

1. Define Investment Objectives:

⟐ **Risk Tolerance:** Determine your risk tolerance and the role of hedge funds within your portfolio. Are you looking for capital preservation, income generation, or capital appreciation?

⟐ **Investment Horizon:** Clarify your investment horizon, whether it's short-term, medium-term, or long-term, as it will influence the choice of hedge fund strategies.

2. Identify Suitable Strategies:

⟐ **Strategy Alignment:** Match hedge fund strategies with your investment objectives. Common strategies include long/short equity, global macro, event-driven, fixed income, and quantitative strategies.

⟐ **Diversification:** Consider diversifying across strategies to reduce risk. A multi-strategy approach can provide a more balanced risk-return profile.

3. Due Diligence Process:

⟐ **Manager Background:** Research the fund manager's background, experience, and track record. Evaluate their expertise in executing the chosen strategy.

⟐ **Performance Analysis:** Assess historical performance, but be cautious of survivorship and backfill biases. Analyze risk-adjusted returns and consistency of performance.

⟐ **Operational Due Diligence:** Investigate the fund's operational infrastructure, including risk management, compliance, and reporting procedures. Verify the fund's transparency and liquidity terms.

⟐ **Fee Structure:** Understand the fee structure, including management fees, performance fees, and any additional costs. Evaluate whether the fees align with the value the fund provides.

4. Risk Assessment:

⟐ **Risk Management:** Evaluate the fund's risk management practices, including position sizing, stop-loss mechanisms, and stress testing. Assess how the fund handles market, credit, and operational risks.

⟐ **Liquidity Analysis:** Analyze the liquidity terms of the fund, including lock-up periods, redemption policies, and gates. Ensure they align with your liquidity needs.

5. Regulatory Compliance:

⟐ **Regulatory Status:** Confirm the fund's regulatory status and compliance with relevant laws and regulations in its jurisdiction.

⟐ **Transparency:** Assess the fund's level of transparency, including disclosure of holdings, reporting frequency, and investor communication.

6. Fund Size and Capacity:

⟐ **Size Considerations:** Consider the fund's size relative to its strategy's capacity. Smaller strategies may perform well with limited capital, while larger funds could face capacity constraints.

⟐ **Investor Base:** Understand the fund's investor base to assess the potential for redemption pressure during market downturns.

7. Qualitative Factors:

⟐ **Manager Philosophy:** Understand the manager's investment philosophy, approach to risk, and alignment with investor interests.

⟐ **Team and Resources:** Evaluate the team's expertise and resources, including research capabilities and access to markets.

8. Ongoing Monitoring:

◈ **Performance Tracking:** Continuously monitor the fund's performance against benchmarks and objectives. Assess whether it continues to meet your investment goals.

◈ **Communication:** Maintain open communication with the fund manager and seek regular updates on strategy and performance.

◈ **Rebalancing:** Rebalance your hedge fund investments periodically to maintain portfolio diversification and risk management.

9. Exit Strategy:

◈ **Redemption Terms:** Familiarize yourself with the fund's redemption terms and exit strategies in case you need to liquidate your investment.

◈ **Contingency Planning:** Have a contingency plan in place for unforeseen circumstances, such as changes in the fund's management or strategy.

Chapter 6: Fund of Hedge Funds (FoHFs) Risk Management

FoHFs Portfolio Construction and Diversification:

Portfolio construction and diversification are fundamental aspects of risk management for Fund of Hedge Funds (FoHFs). FoHFs are unique investment vehicles that allocate capital to a variety of underlying hedge funds. To effectively manage risk and enhance returns, FoHFs must carefully construct their portfolios and diversify across different strategies, managers, and asset classes.

1. Asset Allocation:

◈ **Strategic Allocation:** FoHFs start by setting strategic asset allocation targets based on their investment objectives and risk tolerance. These targets define the desired exposure to various hedge fund strategies and asset classes.

◈ **Tactical Adjustments:** FoHFs may make tactical adjustments to their allocation based on market conditions, changing economic factors, or shifts in investor sentiment. This allows them to capitalize on opportunities and manage risks dynamically.

2. Strategy Selection:

◈ **Diversification:** FoHFs select a mix of hedge fund strategies to diversify risk. Common strategies include long/short equity, global macro, event-driven, and fixed income. Diversification helps reduce the impact of poor performance in any single strategy.

◈ **Risk-Return Profile:** FoHFs evaluate the risk-return profile of each strategy and allocate capital accordingly. They may overweight strategies with higher expected returns and underweight those with lower returns.

3. Manager Selection:

◈ **Due Diligence:** FoHFs conduct thorough due diligence on underlying hedge fund managers. This includes assessing their track records, investment processes, risk management practices, and operational capabilities.

◈ **Manager Diversification:** FoHFs diversify across multiple hedge fund managers within each strategy to reduce manager-specific risk. This approach mitigates the impact of poor performance by any individual manager.

4. Risk Management:

◈ **Risk Budgeting:** FoHFs establish risk budgets for each strategy and manager, specifying acceptable risk levels. This helps ensure that the portfolio's overall risk aligns with investor expectations.

◈ **Risk Monitoring:** FoHFs continuously monitor risk metrics such as volatility, drawdowns, and correlation among underlying funds. If risk limits are breached, they may adjust allocations.

5. Asset Class Diversification:

◈ **Across Asset Classes:** FoHFs diversify across various asset classes beyond hedge funds. These may include traditional assets like equities and fixed income, as well as alternative investments like private equity and real assets. Diversification across asset classes can enhance risk-adjusted returns.

◈ **Uncorrelated Assets:** FoHFs seek to invest in assets with low or negative correlations to hedge fund strategies to reduce portfolio volatility.

6. Geographic Diversification:

◈ **Global Exposure:** FoHFs often seek geographic diversification by investing in hedge funds across different regions and markets. This geographic spread helps mitigate risks associated with regional economic conditions or political events.

7. Liquidity Management:

◈ **Liquidity Needs:** FoHFs consider their investors' liquidity needs and manage the portfolio to meet redemption requests while maintaining exposure to underlying hedge funds.

◈ **Lock-Up Periods:** FoHFs assess the lock-up periods and notice periods of the underlying funds to align with their own liquidity terms.

8. Correlation Analysis:

◈ **Correlation Assessment:** FoHFs conduct correlation analysis to understand how different hedge fund strategies and asset classes interact with each other. Low correlation among investments can enhance diversification.

◈ **Stress Testing:** FoHFs perform stress tests to evaluate portfolio performance under adverse market conditions and identify potential vulnerabilities.

9. Ongoing Monitoring:

◈ **Performance Review:** FoHFs continuously monitor the performance of underlying hedge funds, making adjustments as needed to maintain the desired risk-return profile.

◈ **Rebalancing:** Regular portfolio rebalancing ensures that the allocation to different strategies and managers stays within target ranges.

10. Reporting and Transparency:

◈ **Investor Communication:** FoHFs maintain transparent communication with their investors, providing regular updates on portfolio performance, risk metrics, and any changes to allocation or strategy.

FoHFs employ a structured approach to portfolio construction and diversification to manage risk effectively. By carefully selecting strategies and managers, monitoring risk, and maintaining diversified exposure across asset classes and regions, FoHFs aim to achieve their investment objectives while providing investors with a well-balanced risk-return profile. Successful portfolio construction and diversification are critical for enhancing long-term performance and meeting the expectations of FoHFs' stakeholders.

FoHFs Risk Assessment and Stress Testing:

Risk assessment and stress testing are integral components of effective risk management within Fund of Hedge Funds (FoHFs). These processes help FoHFs evaluate the potential impact of adverse market conditions or unforeseen events on their portfolios, allowing them to make informed decisions and safeguard investors' capital.

1. Risk Identification:

◈ **Asset and Strategy Risks:** FoHFs begin by identifying the various risks associated with the hedge fund strategies and asset classes in their portfolios. These risks may include market risk, credit risk, liquidity risk, and operational risk.

⟐ **Manager Risks:** FoHFs assess the specific risks associated with each underlying hedge fund manager. This includes factors such as manager skill, style drift, and operational vulnerabilities.

2. Quantitative Risk Metrics:

⟐ **Volatility Analysis:** FoHFs utilize metrics like historical and implied volatility to gauge the risk of individual strategies and the entire portfolio. Volatility measures provide insights into potential price fluctuations.

⟐ **Value at Risk (VaR):** FoHFs calculate VaR to estimate the maximum potential loss within a specified confidence interval. VaR helps quantify downside risk.

⟐ **Correlation Analysis:** FoHFs assess the correlation among underlying hedge funds and asset classes to understand how their returns may move in relation to one another. Low correlations are typically sought to enhance diversification.

3. Stress Testing Scenarios:

⟐ **Market Shocks:** FoHFs conduct stress tests by subjecting their portfolios to various market shocks, such as sudden market downturns, interest rate hikes, or extreme volatility. These scenarios simulate adverse conditions.

⟐ **Liquidity Stress:** FoHFs assess their portfolios' resilience to liquidity stress, considering potential redemption requests from investors and the ability to meet those requests without adversely impacting the portfolio's performance.

⟐ **Manager-Specific Events:** FoHFs also model stress scenarios related to specific managers, such as the sudden departure of a key portfolio manager or operational disruptions within a hedge fund.

4. Risk Mitigation Strategies:

◈ **Portfolio Adjustments:** Based on the outcomes of stress tests, FoHFs may make proactive adjustments to their portfolios. This could involve reducing exposure to certain strategies or managers or increasing allocations to strategies that exhibit resilience under stress.

◈ **Hedging Strategies:** FoHFs may employ hedging strategies using derivatives or options to protect against adverse market movements, especially during stress scenarios.

5. Liquidity Risk Management:

◈ **Liquidity Analysis:** FoHFs assess the liquidity profiles of underlying hedge funds, considering lock-up periods and notice periods. This information helps in managing potential redemption risks.

◈ **Cash Reserves:** FoHFs maintain cash reserves or liquid assets to meet redemption requests without the need for forced sales of illiquid assets.

6. Regulatory Compliance:

◈ **Adherence to Regulations:** FoHFs ensure compliance with regulatory requirements related to risk management, reporting, and disclosure. This includes adhering to regulations such as the Alternative Investment Fund Managers Directive (AIFMD) in Europe or the Dodd-Frank Act in the United States.

7. Ongoing Monitoring:

◈ **Regular Risk Review:** FoHFs continuously monitor risk metrics and stress testing results, reviewing and updating their risk management practices as needed.

◈ **Investor Communication:** FoHFs maintain transparent communication with investors, providing insights into the risk assessment process, stress testing outcomes, and risk mitigation strategies.

8. Reporting and Documentation:

◈ **Risk Reports:** FoHFs generate comprehensive risk reports that summarize risk assessment findings, stress test results, and risk mitigation actions. These reports are essential for investor reporting and regulatory compliance.

◈ **Documentation:** FoHFs maintain thorough documentation of their risk management processes, enabling transparency and facilitating audits or regulatory examinations.

Liquidity Management in Fund of Hedge Funds (FoHFs):

Liquidity management is a vital aspect of overseeing a Fund of Hedge Funds (FoHFs) successfully. FoHFs must strike a balance between providing liquidity to investors and managing the illiquidity inherent in many hedge fund investments.

1. Liquidity Profile Assessment:

◈ **Understanding Investor Liquidity Needs:** FoHFs must first understand the liquidity needs and preferences of their investors. Some investors may require more frequent access to their investments, while others may be more patient.

◈ **Liquidity of Underlying Hedge Funds:** FoHFs assess the liquidity profiles of the hedge funds within their portfolio. This includes considering lock-up periods, notice periods, and redemption frequency.

2. Liquidity Sources:

◈ **Cash Reserves:** FoHFs maintain cash reserves to meet regular redemption requests without the need for selling underlying hedge fund assets. This cash buffer ensures that investors can access their funds promptly.

◈ **Line of Credit:** Some FoHFs establish lines of credit with financial institutions to provide additional liquidity in the event of unexpected redemption surges.

3. Redemption Policies:

◈ **Notice Periods:** FoHFs typically have predefined notice periods that investors must adhere to when requesting redemptions. These notice periods allow FoHFs to plan for liquidity needs.

◈ **Gate Provisions:** FoHFs may implement gate provisions that limit the number of redemptions in a given period, often during times of market stress, to protect the interests of remaining investors.

4. Managing Illiquidity:

◈ **Illiquid Assets:** FoHFs often invest in hedge funds with illiquid asset classes, such as private equity or distressed debt. Managing these illiquid assets requires careful planning and coordination.

◈ **Secondary Market Transactions:** FoHFs may explore secondary market transactions to sell illiquid hedge fund positions to other investors or specialized secondary funds.

5. Diversification:

◈ **Asset Class Diversification:** FoHFs diversify their portfolios across various hedge fund strategies and asset classes. This diversification can enhance overall liquidity and reduce the impact of illiquid assets on the portfolio.

6. Stress Testing:

◈ **Scenario Analysis:** FoHFs conduct stress testing and scenario analysis to assess their portfolios' resilience to adverse events, including sudden redemption surges or significant market downturns.

7. Communication:

◈ **Investor Communication:** FoHFs maintain transparent communication with investors regarding liquidity management practices and policies. Clear communication helps set expectations and build trust.

8. Regulatory Compliance:

◈ **Regulatory Requirements:** FoHFs adhere to regulatory requirements related to liquidity management, such as those outlined in the Alternative Investment Fund Managers Directive (AIFMD) in Europe or the Dodd-Frank Act in the United States.

9. Ongoing Monitoring:

◈ **Continuous Assessment:** FoHFs continuously monitor the liquidity profiles of their portfolios and investor redemption patterns. This ongoing assessment allows for adjustments as needed.

10. Documentation:

◈ **Record Keeping:** FoHFs maintain detailed records of liquidity management practices, ensuring transparency and facilitating regulatory compliance.

FoHFs Performance Measurement and Reporting:

Performance measurement and reporting are critical aspects of managing a Fund of Hedge Funds (FoHFs). Investors rely on these metrics to evaluate the FoHFs' ability to generate returns and manage risk effectively.

1. Performance Metrics:

◈ **Absolute Return:** FoHFs measure their performance primarily in terms of absolute returns. This metric reflects the actual gains or losses realized by the FoHFs' investment portfolio.

◈ **Risk-Adjusted Returns:** To provide a more comprehensive view of performance, FoHFs calculate risk-adjusted returns using metrics like the Sharpe ratio, which accounts for the level of risk taken to achieve returns.

2. Benchmarking:

◈ **Selection of Benchmarks:** FoHFs select appropriate benchmarks to compare their performance against. These benchmarks may include broad market indices, hedge fund indices, or customized blended benchmarks that reflect their specific portfolio composition.

◈ **Tracking Error:** FoHFs assess their performance relative to benchmarks by calculating tracking error, which measures the extent to which their returns deviate from those of the benchmark.

3. Attribution Analysis:

◈ **Performance Attribution:** FoHFs conduct attribution analysis to dissect the sources of returns. This analysis helps identify whether returns are primarily driven by manager selection, allocation decisions, or market movements.

4. Risk Reporting:

◈ **Risk Metrics:** FoHFs report various risk metrics, including value at risk (VaR), to provide investors with insights into the potential downside risk associated with the portfolio.

◈ **Stress Testing:** FoHFs perform stress testing to assess how the portfolio may perform under adverse market conditions. This information is crucial for managing risk and setting investor expectations.

5. Transparency:

◈ **Investor Reporting:** FoHFs maintain transparency by providing regular performance reports to investors. These reports include historical performance data, asset allocation details, and risk metrics.

◈ **Client Portals:** Some FoHFs offer online client portals where investors can access real-time performance data and additional information about their investments.

6. Compliance and Regulations:

◈ **Regulatory Compliance:** FoHFs ensure compliance with regulations regarding performance measurement and reporting, such as those outlined in the Alternative Investment Fund Managers Directive (AIFMD) or the Dodd-Frank Act.

7. Investor Relations:

◈ **Client Servicing:** FoHFs have dedicated investor relations teams to address investor inquiries and provide customized reports as needed.

8. Frequency of Reporting:

◈ **Monthly and Quarterly Reports:** FoHFs typically provide monthly or quarterly performance reports to investors. More frequent reporting allows investors to track performance and make informed decisions.

9. Customized Reporting:

◈ **Tailored Reports:** FoHFs may offer customized reporting for institutional investors, catering to specific reporting requirements or benchmarks requested by these clients.

10. Compliance with Global Standards:

◈ **Global Investment Performance Standards (GIPS):** FoHFs may adhere to GIPS standards to ensure consistency and comparability of performance reporting across the industry.

Due Diligence in Selecting Fund of Hedge Funds (FoHFs):

Selecting the right Fund of Hedge Funds (FoHFs) is a crucial step for investors seeking exposure to hedge fund strategies while benefiting from professional portfolio management and risk diversification. Due diligence is a meticulous process that helps investors make informed decisions.

1. Investment Philosophy and Strategy:

◈ **Alignment of Objectives:** Investors assess whether the FoHFs' investment philosophy aligns with their own objectives, risk tolerance, and investment horizon.

◈ **Strategy Suitability:** Due diligence involves evaluating whether the FoHFs' strategies, such as long/short equity, global macro, or fixed income, are well-suited to current market conditions.

2. Manager Selection:

◈ **Manager Expertise:** Evaluating the experience and expertise of the FoHFs' underlying hedge fund managers is critical. Investors consider factors such as track record, investment process, and team qualifications.

◈ **Due Diligence on Underlying Managers:** FoHFs conduct thorough due diligence on the hedge fund managers they select, examining their performance history, risk management practices, and operational infrastructure.

3. Risk Assessment:

◈ **Risk Profile:** Investors assess the FoHFs' risk profile, considering metrics such as value at risk (VaR), historical drawdowns, and correlations with traditional asset classes.

◈ **Liquidity Risk:** Due diligence includes an evaluation of the FoHFs' liquidity management practices, including the ease of redemptions and potential redemption terms.

4. Portfolio Diversification:

◈ **Asset Allocation:** Investors analyze the FoHFs' asset allocation strategy to ensure it aligns with their desired level of diversification and risk exposure.

◈ **Manager Diversification:** Due diligence involves reviewing the FoHFs' selection of underlying managers to assess the diversification benefits across different hedge fund strategies.

5. Fees and Costs:

◈ **Fee Structure:** Investors carefully review the FoHFs' fee structure, considering management fees, performance fees, and any other charges. Understanding the impact of fees on returns is essential.

6. Performance Track Record:

◈ **Historical Returns:** Due diligence includes an evaluation of the FoHFs' historical performance, comparing it to relevant benchmarks and assessing consistency and risk-adjusted returns.

◈ **Survivorship Bias:** Investors account for survivorship bias by considering the performance of both existing and liquidated funds within the FoHFs' track record.

7. Transparency and Reporting:

◈ **Transparency Practices:** Investors assess the FoHFs' transparency regarding underlying hedge fund investments, portfolio holdings, and risk management processes.

◈ **Reporting Quality:** Due diligence includes a review of the quality and frequency of performance reports, as well as the availability of customized reporting for institutional investors.

8. Legal and Compliance:

◈ **Regulatory Compliance:** Investors confirm that the FoHFs adhere to regulatory requirements and industry best practices. This includes compliance with the Alternative Investment Fund Managers Directive (AIFMD), the Dodd-Frank Act, and other relevant regulations.

◈ **Operational Due Diligence:** A comprehensive examination of the FoHFs' operational infrastructure, including valuation practices, trade execution, and risk management procedures, is conducted.

9. Redemption Terms and Liquidity:

◈ **Redemption Provisions:** Investors carefully review the FoHFs' redemption terms, including notice periods and gates, to assess their flexibility and impact on liquidity.

10. Communication and Investor Relations:

◈ **Accessibility:** Investors evaluate the FoHFs' accessibility and responsiveness to inquiries, as well as their willingness to provide information and address investor concerns.

11. Historical Crisis Performance:

⟐ **Performance During Crises:** Due diligence includes an assessment of how FoHFs have performed during previous financial crises or significant market downturns.

12. Peer Comparison:

⟐ **Benchmarking:** Investors may compare the FoHFs with peer group averages and indices to gain insights into relative performance.

13. Ethical Considerations:

⟐ **ESG Integration:** Some investors consider the FoHFs' approach to environmental, social, and governance (ESG) factors in their investment decisions.

Chapter 7: Regulatory Environment for Hedge Funds

In the world of hedge funds, the regulatory environment plays a crucial role in shaping the industry's operations, investor protection, and transparency. The Securities and Exchange Commission (SEC) is one of the primary regulatory bodies overseeing hedge funds and related investment vehicles in the United States.

1. Overview of SEC Regulation:

The Securities and Exchange Commission (SEC) is a federal agency responsible for enforcing securities laws and regulating the securities industry in the United States. It was established in 1934 by the Securities Exchange Act and has since played a pivotal role in overseeing various financial markets and participants, including hedge funds.

2. Registration Requirements:

The SEC has specific registration requirements for hedge funds that meet certain criteria. Hedge fund managers with assets under management (AUM) exceeding a certain threshold are required to register with the SEC as investment advisers. This registration process involves disclosing information about the fund's operations, strategies, key personnel, and potential conflicts of interest.

3. Form ADV:

Hedge fund managers who register with the SEC are mandated to file Form ADV, a document that provides detailed information about the manager's business, investment strategies, fee structure, and any disciplinary history. Form ADV is a critical source of information for investors and regulators to assess the manager's qualifications and operations.

4. Anti-Fraud Provisions:

The SEC enforces anti-fraud provisions under federal securities laws, including the Securities Act of 1933 and the Securities Exchange Act of 1934. Hedge fund managers are prohibited from engaging in fraudulent or deceptive practices, misrepresenting information to investors, or omitting material facts that could impact investment decisions.

5. Insider Trading and Market Manipulation:

The SEC actively investigates and prosecutes insider trading and market manipulation cases related to hedge funds. Hedge fund managers and employees are subject to strict rules regarding the use of non-public information for trading purposes.

6. Investor Protection:

One of the SEC's primary missions is to protect investors. This includes ensuring that hedge fund managers provide accurate and timely information to investors, especially regarding risks associated with the investment.

7. Compliance Programs:

Hedge fund managers subject to SEC regulation are required to establish and maintain compliance programs designed to prevent and detect violations of securities laws. These programs encompass various aspects of fund operations, including risk management, record-keeping, and reporting.

8. Examination and Enforcement:

The SEC conducts examinations and inspections of registered hedge fund managers to assess compliance with securities laws. In cases of non-compliance or violations, the SEC has the authority to take enforcement actions, including fines, sanctions, and revocation of registration.

9. Reporting and Disclosure:

Hedge fund managers registered with the SEC are required to provide periodic reports and disclosures to investors. These reports often include information about the fund's performance, risks, fees, and changes in key personnel.

10. Impact on Hedge Fund Operations:

SEC regulation significantly influences how hedge funds operate. Compliance with regulatory requirements adds administrative burdens and costs to fund managers. However, it also enhances transparency and investor protection, which can attract institutional investors and enhance the industry's credibility.

11. Evolving Regulatory Landscape:

The regulatory landscape for hedge funds continues to evolve. Hedge fund managers must stay abreast of new rules and regulations, such as those related to the Dodd-Frank Wall Street Reform and Consumer Protection Act, and adapt their operations accordingly.

12. Global Implications:

While the SEC primarily regulates hedge funds in the United States, its actions and policies can have global implications. International investors often consider SEC registration and compliance as a sign of good governance and transparency.

Commodity Futures Trading Commission (CFTC) Regulation

In addition to the Securities and Exchange Commission (SEC), the Commodity Futures Trading Commission (CFTC) is another key regulatory body that plays a crucial role in overseeing certain aspects of the hedge fund industry, particularly in relation to commodity futures and derivatives trading.

1. Overview of CFTC Regulation:

The Commodity Futures Trading Commission (CFTC) is a federal agency established in 1974 to regulate commodity futures and options markets in the United States. Its primary mission is to ensure the integrity, transparency, and stability of these markets while protecting market participants from fraud and manipulation.

2. Registration Requirements:

Hedge funds that engage in trading commodity futures contracts and options on futures are subject to registration with the CFTC. This registration is separate from SEC registration and is typically required if a hedge fund's trading activities meet certain thresholds.

3. Commodity Pool Operators (CPOs) and Commodity Trading Advisors (CTAs):

Hedge fund managers who operate commodity pools or provide commodity trading advisory services may need to register as Commodity Pool Operators (CPOs) or Commodity Trading Advisors (CTAs) with the CFTC. These registrations involve disclosing information about their businesses, trading strategies, and key personnel.

4. Disclosure and Reporting:

Registered CPOs and CTAs are required to provide disclosure documents to prospective investors, detailing the fund's investment strategies, risks, and historical performance. They must also report periodically to the CFTC, including information about assets under management, trading activities, and financial condition.

5. Anti-Fraud and Anti-Manipulation Provisions:

The CFTC enforces anti-fraud and anti-manipulation provisions under the Commodity Exchange Act (CEA). Hedge funds are prohibited from engaging in fraudulent activities, such as misrepresenting information about their trading strategies, past performance, or risk profiles.

6. Position Limits and Reporting:

The CFTC sets position limits on certain commodity futures contracts to prevent excessive speculation and market manipulation. Hedge funds that exceed these limits may be subject to reporting requirements and potential enforcement actions.

7. Enforcement and Investigations:

The CFTC conducts investigations and takes enforcement actions against individuals and entities that violate commodities laws and regulations. This includes cases of market manipulation, fraud, and failure to comply with reporting requirements.

8. Clearing and Margin Requirements:

The CFTC regulates the clearing of certain standardized derivatives contracts through central clearinghouses. Hedge funds trading these derivatives may be subject to clearing and margin requirements designed to mitigate systemic risk.

9. Cross-Border Regulation:

The CFTC has been involved in efforts to regulate cross-border activities of hedge funds and other market participants. This includes determining the extraterritorial application of CFTC rules and coordination with international regulatory bodies.

10. Impact on Hedge Fund Operations:

CFTC regulation has a significant impact on hedge funds engaged in commodities trading. Compliance with CFTC rules necessitates adherence to reporting and disclosure requirements, position limits, and margin rules, which can affect the fund's operational processes and costs.

11. Evolving Regulatory Landscape:

Similar to the SEC, the regulatory landscape for hedge funds under CFTC jurisdiction continues to evolve. Hedge fund managers must stay informed about changes in CFTC rules and adapt their trading strategies and operations accordingly.

12. International Implications:

The CFTC's regulatory decisions can have international ramifications, particularly as it cooperates with other global regulators to harmonize rules and promote consistency in the regulation of derivatives markets.

Alternative Investment Fund Managers Directive (AIFMD)

The Alternative Investment Fund Managers Directive (AIFMD) is a European Union (EU) regulatory framework that was introduced to regulate and harmonize the management and marketing of alternative investment funds (AIFs) within the EU. AIFMD has significant implications for hedge funds and other alternative investment managers operating in the European market. Here's an overview of AIFMD and its impact:

1. Background and Purpose:

AIFMD was adopted in 2011 as a response to the global financial crisis to enhance the regulation and supervision of AIFs and their managers. The directive aims to provide a comprehensive regulatory framework for AIFs to protect investors, ensure market stability, and facilitate the cross-border marketing of AIFs within the EU.

2. Regulatory Scope:

AIFMD applies to a wide range of alternative investment funds, including hedge funds, private equity funds, real estate funds, and more. It also covers fund managers, known as Alternative Investment Fund Managers (AIFMs), who manage and market these funds.

3. Authorization and Supervision:

Under AIFMD, AIFMs are required to obtain authorization from their home member state's regulatory authority to operate within the EU. Once authorized, AIFMs are subject to ongoing supervision and regulatory reporting.

4. Depositaries:

AIFMD mandates the appointment of a depositary for each AIF. The depositary's role is to safeguard the fund's assets, verify ownership, and ensure compliance with AIFMD rules. This is an important investor protection measure.

5. Transparency and Reporting:

AIFMs are required to provide investors with detailed information about the AIF's strategy, risks, and fees through a standardized document called the "Key Information Document" (KID). AIFMs must also report to regulatory authorities on matters such as risk exposures, leverage, and liquidity management.

6. Marketing Passport:

AIFMD introduced a marketing passport that allows AIFMs authorized in one EU member state to market their AIFs to professional investors throughout the EU without the need for separate authorizations in each member state. This simplifies cross-border fund marketing.

7. Third-Country Regimes:

AIFMD also addresses the marketing of AIFs from non-EU countries (third countries). It provides a framework for the marketing of AIFs from third countries to professional investors in the EU, subject to certain conditions and cooperation agreements between regulators.

8. Remuneration Rules:

AIFMD includes rules on the remuneration of AIFM staff, aimed at aligning remuneration structures with long-term fund performance and discouraging excessive risk-taking.

9. Impact on Hedge Funds:

Hedge fund managers operating in the EU or marketing to EU investors must comply with AIFMD's provisions. This includes obtaining authorization, appointing depositaries, providing transparent disclosures, and adhering to remuneration rules.

10. Evolving Landscape:

AIFMD is not static; it has undergone amendments and refinements since its inception. Hedge fund managers need to stay current with regulatory developments and adapt their operations and compliance practices accordingly.

11. Compliance Challenges:

Complying with AIFMD can be complex and costly for hedge fund managers, particularly smaller firms. Meeting reporting requirements and navigating the nuances of cross-border marketing can pose challenges.

12. Industry Impact:

AIFMD has had a significant impact on the alternative investment industry in Europe, influencing fund structuring, distribution strategies, and operational practices.

Alternative Investment Fund Managers Directive (AIFMD) is a comprehensive regulatory framework that affects hedge funds and other alternative investment managers operating in the European Union. It introduces authorization and reporting requirements, depositary oversight, and remuneration rules, with the goal of enhancing investor protection and market stability while facilitating cross-border fund marketing within the EU. Hedge fund managers operating in or marketing to the EU must carefully navigate AIFMD compliance to operate successfully in this regulatory landscape.

Dodd-Frank Act and Reporting Requirements

The Dodd-Frank Wall Street Reform and Consumer Protection Act, commonly known as the Dodd-Frank Act, is a comprehensive financial reform law enacted in the United States in 2010 in response to the 2008 financial crisis. It introduced a wide range of regulatory changes to promote financial stability, protect consumers, and increase transparency in the financial markets. One of its key aspects is reporting requirements, which have a significant impact on hedge funds and other financial institutions. Here's an overview of the Dodd-Frank Act and its reporting requirements:

1. Background and Purpose:

The Dodd-Frank Act was enacted to address the vulnerabilities and regulatory gaps that contributed to the financial crisis of 2008. Its primary objectives include reducing systemic risk, enhancing transparency, and protecting consumers from abusive financial practices.

2. Registration and Regulation:

Under the Dodd-Frank Act, certain hedge funds and private equity firms that meet specific criteria are required to register with the U.S. Securities and Exchange Commission (SEC) as investment advisers. This registration process subjects them to various reporting and compliance requirements.

3. Form PF Reporting:

One of the significant reporting requirements introduced by Dodd-Frank is the filing of Form PF (Private Fund), which is submitted to the SEC by registered investment advisers managing private funds, including hedge funds. Form PF is designed to collect detailed information about a fund's strategy, assets under management (AUM), leverage, risk exposures, and performance. It aims to assist regulatory agencies in monitoring systemic risk in the financial system.

4. Systemically Important Financial Institutions (SIFIs):

Dodd-Frank established the Financial Stability Oversight Council (FSOC) to identify and designate certain financial institutions, including non-bank financial companies like hedge funds, as Systemically Important Financial Institutions (SIFIs). SIFIs are subject to enhanced regulatory oversight by the Federal Reserve and must adhere to additional reporting and risk management requirements.

5. Volcker Rule Compliance:

The Dodd-Frank Act includes the Volcker Rule, which restricts proprietary trading and certain investment activities by banking entities and their affiliates. Hedge funds that are affiliated with banking entities are subject to Volcker Rule compliance, which may involve reporting and record-keeping obligations.

6. Reporting of Swaps and Derivatives:

Dodd-Frank introduced significant reforms to the derivatives market. Hedge funds engaging in derivatives trading are required to report certain swap transactions to swap data repositories (SDRs). These reports enhance market transparency and provide regulators with real-time data on derivatives trading activities.

7. Record-Keeping and Compliance Programs:

Hedge funds and other financial institutions are required to maintain records and establish compliance programs to ensure adherence to various Dodd-Frank provisions. This includes documenting risk management practices, trading activities, and compliance with reporting requirements.

8. Consumer Protection Measures:

While the primary focus of Dodd-Frank is on financial stability and market oversight, it also contains provisions aimed at protecting consumers from predatory lending practices, abusive financial products, and unfair business practices.

9. Ongoing Regulatory Developments:

Dodd-Frank has been subject to ongoing regulatory developments and rulemaking by various U.S. regulatory agencies, including the SEC, CFTC, and the Federal Reserve. Hedge funds must stay current with these evolving regulations and adapt their compliance practices accordingly.

10. Industry Impact:

The Dodd-Frank Act has had a profound impact on the hedge fund industry, increasing regulatory scrutiny and compliance costs. It has also led to greater transparency in hedge fund operations and risk management practices.

Dodd-Frank Act introduced extensive reporting and regulatory requirements that affect hedge funds and other financial institutions operating in the United States. These requirements aim to enhance financial stability, promote transparency, and protect consumers from abusive financial practices. Hedge fund managers must navigate these compliance obligations to operate successfully in the post-Dodd-Frank regulatory landscape.

Global Regulatory Trends and Initiatives

Global regulatory trends and initiatives have a significant impact on the hedge fund industry, as hedge funds operate in a globalized financial landscape where regulatory standards and practices are increasingly interconnected. Here's an in-depth exploration of global regulatory trends and initiatives that influence hedge funds:

1. International Coordination:

Regulatory authorities around the world are increasingly coordinating their efforts to address cross-border financial market challenges. Initiatives like the Financial Stability Board (FSB) aim to promote global financial stability by identifying and addressing systemic risks. Hedge funds often operate in multiple jurisdictions, and international coordination helps harmonize regulatory standards.

2. Anti-Money Laundering (AML) and Know Your Customer (KYC) Requirements:

Global regulators have strengthened AML and KYC requirements to combat money laundering, terrorist financing, and fraud. Hedge funds must implement robust AML and KYC procedures to comply with these regulations and mitigate associated risks.

3. Common Reporting Standards (CRS):

CRS, developed by the Organisation for Economic Co-operation and Development (OECD), aims to combat offshore tax evasion by requiring financial institutions, including hedge funds, to report financial account information of foreign account holders to their respective tax authorities. Hedge funds with international investors must adhere to CRS requirements.

4. MiFID II and MiFIR:

The Markets in Financial Instruments Directive (MiFID II) and the Markets in Financial Instruments Regulation (MiFIR) in the European Union have introduced extensive regulations governing the trading and reporting of financial instruments. Hedge funds conducting business in the EU must comply with these rules, impacting their trading practices, transaction reporting, and transparency requirements.

5. GDPR Compliance:

The General Data Protection Regulation (GDPR) is a comprehensive data protection regulation in the European Union. Hedge funds collecting and processing personal data of EU residents must comply with GDPR's strict data protection and privacy requirements.

6. Basel III:

Basel III is a global regulatory framework for banking supervision that includes capital and liquidity requirements. While it primarily applies to banks, its impact trickles down to hedge funds through counterparty risk and capital allocation considerations.

7. ESG and Sustainable Finance Initiatives:

Environmental, Social, and Governance (ESG) considerations are increasingly integrated into financial regulation. Regulators are promoting sustainable finance practices, and hedge funds are encouraged to incorporate ESG factors into their investment strategies and reporting.

8. FATCA Compliance:

The Foreign Account Tax Compliance Act (FATCA) requires foreign financial institutions, including hedge funds, to report financial accounts held by U.S. taxpayers to the Internal Revenue Service (IRS). Hedge funds operating globally must comply with FATCA's reporting requirements.

9. Cybersecurity Regulations:

Regulators globally are emphasizing cybersecurity standards to protect financial systems and data from cyber threats. Hedge funds must implement robust cybersecurity measures and reporting mechanisms to safeguard their operations.

10. Impact of Brexit:

The United Kingdom's departure from the European Union (Brexit) has introduced regulatory changes and uncertainties. Hedge funds with operations in the UK and the EU must navigate evolving regulatory landscapes and consider their market access and compliance obligations.

11. Sustainable Finance Disclosure Regulation (SFDR):

The SFDR in the European Union requires financial market participants, including hedge funds, to disclose the sustainability-related information of their investments. Hedge funds need to integrate sustainability considerations into their investment strategies and report on their sustainability objectives.

Hedge funds operate in a dynamic global regulatory environment influenced by various trends and initiatives. To remain compliant and competitive, hedge funds must closely monitor and adapt to these evolving regulatory landscapes, implement robust compliance programs, and engage with regulators and industry associations to stay informed about best practices and standards. Global regulatory trends and initiatives continue to shape the operational and reporting requirements for hedge funds worldwide.

Chapter 8: Alternative Investment Strategies

Managed Futures and Commodity Trading Advisors (CTAs)

Managed futures and Commodity Trading Advisors (CTAs) are alternative investment strategies that offer distinct approaches to portfolio diversification and potential returns.

1. Managed Futures Strategies:

◈ **Definition:** Managed futures involve investing in futures contracts across various asset classes, including commodities, currencies, interest rates, and equity indices.

◈ **Investment Approach:** Managed futures managers actively trade futures contracts with the goal of profiting from price trends, whether upward (long positions) or downward (short positions).

◈ **Diversification Benefits:** Managed futures provide diversification because their returns often have low correlations with traditional asset classes like stocks and bonds. This can enhance a portfolio's risk-adjusted returns.

◈ **Risk Management:** Risk management is crucial in managed futures, with managers employing techniques such as position sizing, stop-loss orders, and portfolio rebalancing to manage risk.

2. Commodity Trading Advisors (CTAs):

◈ **Definition:** CTAs are investment professionals or firms that manage portfolios of futures and options contracts, primarily in commodities but also in other asset classes.

◈ **Investment Approach:** CTAs use quantitative models and technical analysis to make trading decisions in futures markets. They may employ trend-following, mean-reversion, or systematic trading strategies.

◈ **Diversification Benefits:** CTAs offer diversification by accessing commodities markets, which have historically shown low correlations with traditional investments. This can help reduce overall portfolio risk.

◈ **Risk Management:** CTAs are diligent about risk management, often employing stop-loss mechanisms, portfolio diversification, and position sizing to limit potential losses.

3. Historical Performance:

◈ Historically, managed futures and CTAs have demonstrated the potential for attractive returns, particularly during periods of market turbulence and economic uncertainty.

◈ Their performance can be cyclical, with periods of strong returns followed by periods of underperformance. Investors should consider their investment horizon and risk tolerance.

4. Accessing Managed Futures and CTAs:

◈ Investors can access managed futures and CTAs through managed futures funds or separately managed accounts (SMAs). SMAs offer greater customization but may have higher investment minimums.

◈ Due diligence is essential when selecting managed futures managers or CTAs. Investors should evaluate track records, trading strategies, risk management procedures, and fees.

5. Risks and Considerations:

◈ Managed futures and CTAs are not risk-free investments. They can be volatile, and investors may experience drawdowns during challenging market conditions.

◈ High fees are often associated with managed futures and CTAs, including management fees and performance-based fees. These costs can erode returns.

6. Regulatory Considerations:

◈ Managed futures and CTAs are subject to regulatory oversight, primarily by the Commodity Futures Trading Commission (CFTC) in the United States.

◈ Compliance with regulatory requirements, including reporting and transparency, is essential for CTAs and managed futures managers.

7. Role in Portfolio Allocation:

◈ Managed futures and CTAs can play a role in portfolio allocation as diversification tools. They offer non-correlated returns and can enhance overall portfolio risk-adjusted returns.

◈ The allocation to managed futures and CTAs should align with an investor's risk tolerance and long-term objectives.

Managed futures and Commodity Trading Advisors (CTAs) are alternative investment strategies that offer diversification benefits and potential returns by trading futures contracts across various asset classes. Investors considering these strategies should conduct thorough due diligence, understand the risks involved, and assess their compatibility with their overall investment goals and risk tolerance.

Private Equity and Venture Capital

Private Equity (PE) and Venture Capital (VC) are distinct yet related alternative investment strategies that focus on investing in private companies.

1. Private Equity (PE):

◈ **Definition:** Private equity refers to investments made in private companies, typically through the acquisition of equity (ownership) stakes. PE firms raise capital from institutional investors and high-net-worth individuals to invest in and manage private businesses.

◈ **Investment Approach:** PE firms seek to create value in their portfolio companies through various strategies, such as operational improvements, cost reductions, and strategic initiatives. They often take an active role in managing their investments.

◈ **Types of Investments:** PE investments can take the form of buyouts (acquiring a controlling stake in an existing company), growth capital (investing in established companies to fuel expansion), or distressed asset purchases.

◈ **Exit Strategies:** PE firms typically have a predefined exit strategy, aiming to sell or take their portfolio companies public (initial public offering, IPO) within a certain investment horizon, usually 3-7 years.

2. Venture Capital (VC):

◈ **Definition:** Venture capital involves investing in early-stage and high-growth companies that have the potential for significant expansion. VC funds are typically raised from institutional investors and wealthy individuals.

◈ **Investment Approach:** VC firms provide capital, mentorship, and expertise to startups in exchange for equity. They actively support the growth and development of these companies.

◈ **Stages of Investment:** VC investments are often categorized into stages, including seed funding, Series A, Series B, and so on, based on the company's development and funding needs.

◈ **Exit Strategies:** VC investors seek exits through acquisitions by larger companies or IPOs. The aim is to realize substantial returns on their investments.

3. Role in Entrepreneurship and Innovation:

◈ VC plays a pivotal role in fostering innovation and entrepreneurship by providing early-stage capital to startups with groundbreaking ideas.

◈ PE firms often invest in more mature companies, helping them scale and become more competitive in their respective industries.

4. Risks and Returns:

◈ Both PE and VC investments carry inherent risks due to the illiquid nature of private markets. Returns can be substantial but may take years to materialize.

◈ The risk-return profile varies within each category; for instance, early-stage VC investments are riskier but may offer higher potential returns.

5. Portfolio Diversification:

◈ PE and VC can be used to diversify a traditional investment portfolio. Their returns may have low correlations with public equity markets, providing risk-reduction benefits.

6. Regulatory Framework:

⟐ Regulatory oversight varies by region and can impact the operations and fundraising activities of PE and VC firms. Compliance with securities laws and reporting requirements is crucial.

7. Due Diligence and Selection:

⟐ Investors in PE and VC should conduct thorough due diligence on fund managers, assessing track records, investment strategies, and alignment of interests.

⟐ VC investors often seek startups with disruptive technologies, strong teams, and scalable business models.

8. Ethical Considerations:

⟐ Both PE and VC industries are increasingly focused on ethical investing, environmental, social, and governance (ESG) criteria, and sustainability.

9. Case Studies:

⟐ Illustrative case studies can showcase successful PE and VC investments, highlighting the strategies and factors that contributed to their success.

Private Equity (PE) and Venture Capital (VC) are dynamic investment strategies that play vital roles in fostering innovation, supporting entrepreneurs, and creating value in private companies. Understanding their nuances, risk profiles, and potential returns is essential for investors considering allocation to these alternative asset classes. Careful due diligence and alignment with investment objectives are key to successful participation in PE and VC investments.

Real Assets and Infrastructure Investments

Real assets and infrastructure investments are essential components of alternative investment portfolios.

1. Real Assets:

◈ **Definition:** Real assets encompass a broad category of tangible investments, including real estate, natural resources (e.g., timber, agriculture), and infrastructure. These assets have intrinsic value and may provide income and potential for capital appreciation.

◈ **Investment Objectives:** Real assets are often included in portfolios to provide diversification, inflation protection, and income generation. They can serve as hedges against economic uncertainty.

◈ **Real Estate:** Investing in physical properties, such as residential, commercial, industrial, and hospitality real estate.

◈ **Natural Resources:** Investing in assets like timberland, farmland, and mineral rights.

◈ **Infrastructure:** Investments in essential infrastructure projects like airports, roads, bridges, utilities, and renewable energy facilities.

2. Infrastructure Investments:

◈ **Definition:** Infrastructure investments involve financing, developing, or owning physical assets that provide essential services to communities and businesses. Infrastructure can be categorized as social (e.g., hospitals, schools) or economic (e.g., transportation, energy).

◈ **Investment Approach:** Infrastructure investments often offer stable, long-term cash flows with the potential for inflation-linked returns. They can be made directly in assets or through infrastructure funds.

◈ **Types of Infrastructure:** Examples include transportation (e.g., airports, ports, toll roads), energy (e.g., power generation, utilities), social infrastructure (e.g., schools, hospitals), and digital infrastructure (e.g., data centers, communication networks).

◈ **Risk and Regulation:** Regulatory frameworks, government policies, and geopolitical factors can significantly impact the risk-return profile of infrastructure investments.

3. Role in Portfolio Diversification:

◈ Real assets and infrastructure investments are known for their low correlation with traditional asset classes, making them valuable tools for portfolio diversification.

◈ They can provide stability and consistent income streams, particularly in volatile markets.

4. Challenges and Considerations:

◈ Due diligence is crucial when investing in physical assets, as they require maintenance, management, and adherence to regulations.

◈ Real assets and infrastructure investments may have high upfront costs, long investment horizons, and liquidity constraints.

5. Ethical and Sustainable Investing:

◈ Investors are increasingly considering environmental, social, and governance (ESG) factors in real asset and infrastructure investments.

◈ Sustainability and responsible investing practices are essential considerations in these asset classes.

6. Case Studies:

◈ Highlighting successful real asset and infrastructure investments, including those with positive environmental and social impacts.

7. Regulatory Landscape:

◈ Overview of regulations and policies governing real asset and infrastructure investments, including tax incentives and government partnerships.

8. Future Trends:

◈ Exploration of emerging trends such as investments in renewable energy infrastructure, digital infrastructure, and the evolving role of public-private partnerships.

Real assets and infrastructure investments offer diversification benefits, income potential, and a hedge against inflation. They play pivotal roles in addressing infrastructure needs and fostering sustainable development. Investors should conduct thorough due diligence, consider the regulatory landscape, and align investments with their financial objectives and ethical considerations when participating in these alternative asset classes.

Distressed Debt and Special Situations

Distressed debt and special situations are niche alternative investment strategies that can provide unique opportunities and challenges.

1. Distressed Debt:

◈ **Definition:** Distressed debt refers to bonds or loans issued by companies that are experiencing financial distress or are in or near bankruptcy. These securities often trade at significant discounts due to the increased risk of default.

◈ **Investment Objectives:** Investors in distressed debt seek to profit from the potential recovery of these securities as the distressed company's financial condition improves.

◈ **Strategies:** Distressed debt strategies may involve investing in various debt instruments, including senior secured debt, unsecured debt, and distressed equity (equity of companies in bankruptcy or near bankruptcy).

◈ **Due Diligence:** Rigorous financial analysis and legal expertise are essential for evaluating the distressed company's prospects and understanding the complex legal structures of distressed securities.

2. Special Situations:

◈ **Definition:** Special situations encompass a wide range of event-driven investment opportunities, including mergers and acquisitions, corporate restructurings, spin-offs, and other unique events.

◈ **Investment Approach:** Special situations investors aim to profit from mispricings or inefficiencies created by specific corporate events or market conditions.

◈ **Examples:** Special situations can involve investing in companies undergoing mergers, acquisitions, or divestitures; participating in rights offerings; or capitalizing on spin-offs and other corporate actions.

3. Role in Portfolio Diversification:

◈ Distressed debt and special situations investments can offer low correlation with traditional asset classes, making them valuable for portfolio diversification.

◈ They provide an opportunity to generate returns that are less dependent on broader market trends.

4. Challenges and Risks:

◈ Distressed debt investing carries inherent credit and default risks, and the outcome can be uncertain, depending on the distressed company's ability to recover.

◈ Special situations investments require a deep understanding of the specific event and may involve regulatory and legal complexities.

5. Ethical Considerations:

◈ Investors should consider the ethical implications of investing in distressed debt, particularly when it involves companies facing severe financial distress.

6. Case Studies:

◈ Highlighting successful distressed debt and special situations investments, illustrating the strategies and outcomes.

7. Regulatory Environment:

◈ Overview of regulatory considerations and potential legal constraints in distressed debt and special situations investing.

8. Future Trends:

◈ Exploration of emerging trends, such as the impact of changing bankruptcy laws and regulations, and the evolving landscape of special situations investing.

Distressed debt and special situations investing offer unique opportunities to capitalize on market inefficiencies and corporate events. These strategies require in-depth research, legal expertise, and a thorough understanding of the risks involved. As part of a diversified portfolio, they can contribute to overall returns and risk mitigation. However, investors should carefully assess the ethical implications and remain informed about regulatory developments in this dynamic investment space.

Global Macro and Emerging Markets Strategies

Global Macro and Emerging Markets strategies are distinct investment approaches that focus on macroeconomic factors and opportunities in emerging economies.

1. Global Macro Strategies:

◈ **Definition:** Global macro strategies involve making investment decisions based on macroeconomic and geopolitical analysis. Fund managers take positions in various asset classes, including currencies, bonds, equities, and commodities, to profit from macroeconomic trends and events.

◈ **Investment Objectives:** The primary goal is to generate positive returns by correctly anticipating and capitalizing on global macroeconomic developments.

◈ **Strategies:** Global macro managers use a top-down approach, considering factors such as interest rates, inflation, central bank policies, and political events to make investment decisions.

◈ **Risk Management:** Risk management is crucial in global macro investing, as positions can be highly leveraged and volatile.

2. Emerging Markets Strategies:

◈ **Definition:** Emerging markets strategies focus on investments in developing or emerging economies, which often have higher growth potential but also higher risks compared to developed markets.

◈ **Investment Approach:** Investors seek opportunities in equity markets, fixed income, private equity, and other asset classes within emerging markets.

◈ **Strategies:** Emerging markets strategies may include targeting specific countries or regions, investing in companies poised for growth, or participating in infrastructure development.

◈ **Risks and Rewards:** Emerging markets offer the potential for significant returns, but they also come with political, currency, and liquidity risks.

3. Portfolio Diversification:

◈ Both global macro and emerging markets strategies can enhance portfolio diversification by providing exposure to different markets and asset classes.

◈ Investors can benefit from reduced correlation with traditional assets, potentially improving risk-adjusted returns.

4. Challenges and Risks:

◈ Global macro strategies require accurate macroeconomic forecasting, which is inherently challenging.

◈ Emerging markets investments can be volatile and subject to regulatory changes, currency fluctuations, and geopolitical events.

5. Ethical Considerations:

◈ Investors in emerging markets should consider ethical factors, such as environmental and social responsibilities, when evaluating investment opportunities.

6. Case Studies:

◈ Examining successful global macro and emerging markets investments to illustrate strategies, challenges, and outcomes.

7. Regulatory Environment:

◈ Discussion of regulatory considerations specific to global macro and emerging markets investing, including currency controls and foreign investment restrictions.

8. Future Trends:

◈ Exploration of emerging trends, such as the role of technology in emerging markets, and the impact of global economic shifts on global macro strategies.

Global macro and emerging markets strategies offer investors the potential for attractive returns by capitalizing on macroeconomic trends and emerging market opportunities. However, these strategies require a deep understanding of macroeconomics, thorough research, and risk management. As part of a diversified portfolio, they can contribute to returns and provide diversification benefits. Investors should also be aware of the unique challenges and ethical considerations associated with these strategies while staying informed about regulatory developments.

Chapter 9: Hedge Funds and Portfolio Diversification

Correlation Analysis Defined:

◈ **Definition:** Correlation analysis is a statistical method used to measure the degree to which the returns of two or more assets move in relation to each other. It quantifies the relationship between hedge funds and traditional asset classes like stocks, bonds, and real estate.

◈ **Importance:** Understanding the correlation between hedge funds and traditional assets is crucial for constructing a diversified portfolio that can help mitigate risk and enhance returns.

2. Benefits of Low Correlation:

◈ **Risk Reduction:** Hedge funds with low correlations to traditional asset classes can act as a risk-reducing component in a portfolio. When traditional assets decline, low-correlation hedge funds may provide a buffer.

◈ **Return Enhancement:** By adding assets with low correlation, investors can potentially enhance the risk-adjusted returns of their portfolios.

3. Diversification Strategies:

◈ **Asset Allocation:** The chapter delves into strategies for allocating assets across hedge funds and traditional asset classes, aiming for an optimal risk-return profile.

◈ **Risk Parity:** Exploring risk parity strategies that balance risk across different asset classes, including hedge funds, to achieve diversification.

4. Risk Factors and Factors Driving Correlation:

⦿ Discussing various risk factors that can affect the correlation between hedge funds and traditional assets. These factors include market conditions, economic cycles, and specific hedge fund strategies.

⦿ Factors driving correlation, such as systemic risks or market sentiment, are examined.

5. Analyzing Historical Data:

⦿ Analyzing historical data to illustrate how hedge fund strategies have correlated with traditional asset classes during different market environments, including bull and bear markets.

6. Portfolio Construction:

⦿ Practical guidance on constructing portfolios that incorporate hedge funds to achieve desired risk and return objectives.

7. Case Studies:

⦿ Presenting case studies that showcase the impact of hedge funds on portfolio diversification in real-world scenarios. These studies can provide insights into how hedge funds have historically influenced portfolio performance.

8. Challenges and Considerations:

⦿ Discussing challenges related to hedge fund investing, such as liquidity risk and the potential for changing correlations during market crises.

⦿ Highlighting the importance of due diligence when selecting hedge fund managers.

9. Ethical and ESG Considerations:

◈ Examining the ethical and environmental, social, and governance (ESG) considerations in hedge fund investing and how these factors may affect correlation analysis.

10. Regulatory Implications:

◈ Exploring how regulatory changes, such as reporting requirements or restrictions on certain strategies, can impact the correlation between hedge funds and traditional assets.

11. Future Trends:

◈ Looking ahead to emerging trends in hedge fund investing and how these trends may affect correlation dynamics with traditional asset classes.

Understanding the relationship between hedge funds and traditional assets is essential for optimizing risk-adjusted returns and achieving investment goals. It also acknowledges the challenges, ethical considerations, regulatory factors, and future trends that shape the landscape of hedge fund investing and its role in portfolio diversification.

1. Risk Parity Defined:

◈ **Definition:** Risk parity is an asset allocation strategy that aims to balance the risk contributed by different asset classes in a portfolio. It focuses on allocating capital based on the volatility or risk associated with each asset class rather than traditional methods like equal-weighting or market capitalization.

2. Principles of Risk Parity:

◈ **Balanced Risk:** The primary principle is to ensure that each asset class contributes equally to the overall portfolio risk. This means that asset allocation is adjusted to achieve this balance.

◈ **Diversification:** Risk parity promotes diversification across a range of asset classes, including hedge funds, equities, fixed income, and other alternatives.

3. Hedge Funds in Risk Parity:

◈ **Inclusion:** The chapter discusses the role of hedge funds as a component of a risk parity strategy. Hedge funds are considered for their potential to provide uncorrelated returns and reduce overall portfolio risk.

◈ **Diversification Benefits:** It explores how hedge funds, with their wide range of strategies, can contribute to the diversification goals of a risk parity portfolio.

4. Portfolio Construction:

◈ **Asset Allocation:** The chapter provides insights into the process of allocating assets in a risk parity portfolio, considering the risk profiles of each asset class.

◈ **Weighting Schemes:** Different weighting schemes, including risk-based weighting, are examined to achieve balanced risk contributions.

5. Risk Assessment and Management:

◈ **Risk Metrics:** The use of risk metrics, such as volatility and correlation, to assess and manage risk in a risk parity portfolio. It discusses how these metrics are applied to hedge funds.

◈ **Stress Testing:** The importance of stress testing to evaluate how a risk parity portfolio may perform under adverse market conditions, including stress scenarios involving hedge fund strategies.

6. Historical Performance:

◈ **Analysis:** The chapter may include historical performance analysis, showing how risk parity portfolios with hedge funds have performed in various market environments compared to traditional portfolios.

◈ **Case Studies:** Real-world case studies that demonstrate the effectiveness of risk parity strategies with hedge fund allocations.

7. Challenges and Considerations:

◈ **Liquidity Management:** Discussing the challenge of managing liquidity in risk parity portfolios, especially when including less liquid hedge fund investments.

◈ **Manager Selection:** Highlighting the importance of due diligence when selecting hedge fund managers for a risk parity strategy.

8. Regulatory Implications:

◈ **Regulatory Compliance:** Addressing how regulatory requirements can impact the implementation of risk parity strategies, especially concerning hedge fund investments.

9. Ethical and ESG Considerations:

◈ **Ethical Investing:** Examining whether risk parity strategies align with ethical and environmental, social, and governance (ESG) considerations, and the role of hedge funds in ESG-focused portfolios.

10. Future Trends:

◈ **Emerging Trends:** Looking ahead to emerging trends in risk parity strategies and the evolving role of hedge funds within these strategies.

It emphasizes the importance of achieving balanced risk contributions across asset classes and discusses the benefits, challenges, and considerations associated with incorporating hedge funds into risk parity portfolios. Real-world examples, performance analysis, and future trends contribute to a comprehensive understanding of risk parity and its relationship with hedge funds.

1. Institutional Portfolio Management:

⟐ **Definition:** Institutional portfolios typically manage assets on behalf of organizations such as pension funds, endowments, and foundations. This section outlines the unique characteristics and objectives of institutional portfolio management.

2. Role of Hedge Funds:

⟐ **Inclusion Rationale:** The chapter discusses why institutional investors consider incorporating hedge funds into their portfolios. This may include potential for uncorrelated returns, risk mitigation, and diversification benefits.

3. Due Diligence and Selection:

⟐ **Manager Selection:** The chapter covers the rigorous due diligence process that institutional investors undertake when selecting hedge fund managers. This involves assessing factors such as track record, strategy, risk management, and operational infrastructure.

⟐ **Funds of Hedge Funds:** Discussion of the use of funds of hedge funds (FoHFs) by institutions as a way to access a diversified portfolio of hedge funds.

4. Risk Management in Institutional Portfolios:

⟐ **Risk Allocation:** How institutional portfolios allocate risk across asset classes, including hedge funds, to achieve their specific risk-return objectives.

⟐ **Risk Monitoring:** Tools and processes for monitoring and managing risk within institutional portfolios, with a focus on hedge fund risk.

5. Optimal Allocation Models:

⟐ **Portfolio Optimization:** Explanation of various portfolio optimization models used by institutional investors to determine the optimal allocation to hedge funds. These models consider factors such as risk tolerance, return expectations, and correlation analysis.

⟐ **Efficient Frontier:** Discussion of how institutional investors seek to construct portfolios along the efficient frontier, balancing risk and return through the inclusion of hedge funds.

6. Performance Evaluation:

⟐ **Performance Metrics:** An examination of performance evaluation metrics tailored to institutional portfolios with hedge fund allocations. This may include the Sharpe ratio, information ratio, and benchmarks.

⟐ **Attribution Analysis:** Insights into how institutional investors conduct performance attribution analysis to understand the drivers of hedge fund performance.

7. Liquidity Management:

⟐ **Liquidity Needs:** How institutional investors manage liquidity requirements when incorporating hedge funds into their portfolios, including considerations of redemption terms and lock-up periods.

8. Regulatory and Compliance Considerations:

⟐ **Regulatory Compliance:** Addressing regulatory and compliance requirements that impact institutional portfolios investing in hedge funds, including reporting and transparency.

9. Ethical and ESG Considerations:

◈ **Ethical Investing:** Exploring whether institutional portfolios take ethical and ESG factors into account when allocating to hedge funds and the role of hedge funds in ESG-focused portfolios.

10. Case Studies and Real-World Examples:

◈ **Practical Application:** The chapter may include case studies and real-world examples of institutional portfolios successfully incorporating hedge funds, demonstrating the benefits and challenges faced.

11. Future Trends:

◈ **Emerging Trends:** Discussion of emerging trends in institutional hedge fund allocation, including evolving strategies, technology adoption, and the integration of alternative data.

Chapter 10: Ethical Considerations in Hedge Funds

In the final chapter of our comprehensive exploration of hedge funds, we delve into the critical realm of ethical considerations that define the industry. Ethics, while often taken for granted in the financial world, form the bedrock upon which the reputation and trustworthiness of hedge funds are built. It is here that we examine the nuanced ethical terrain, navigate the ethical dilemmas, and outline the best practices that guide hedge funds in their pursuit of financial success while maintaining the highest ethical standards.

1. Hedge Fund Industry Ethics and Best Practices:

◈ **Ethical Framework:** At the outset, we establish a robust ethical framework. This framework highlights that ethics should not merely be a compliance requirement but an integral part of a hedge fund's DNA. Ethical conduct isn't just about staying on the right side of the law; it's about doing what's right for clients and the broader financial ecosystem.

◈ **Industry Standards:** We delve into the industry standards that set the bar for hedge funds, including codes of conduct and best practices. These standards, often set by industry associations and regulatory bodies, define the ethical expectations within the sector.

2. Insider Trading and Market Manipulation:

◈ **Insider Trading:** Insider trading stands at the crossroads of legality and ethics. We explore the ethical dimensions of possessing non-public information and the importance of respecting the legal boundaries that separate legitimate research from illegal insider trading.

◈ **Market Manipulation:** Market manipulation, including activities like pump-and-dump schemes, presents complex ethical challenges. We discuss the ethical concerns associated with these practices and how hedge funds can uphold their ethical responsibilities in a competitive marketplace.

3. Hedge Fund Activism and Corporate Governance:

◈ **Shareholder Activism:** Shareholder activism can be a force for positive change, but it also poses ethical questions. We examine the ethical dilemmas surrounding shareholder activism and the responsibilities that hedge funds bear in advocating for corporate change.

◈ **Proxy Battles:** Proxy battles often turn into high-stakes ethical showdowns. We dissect the ethical considerations when hedge funds engage in corporate governance disputes and how they can balance their fiduciary duties with ethical principles.

4. Socially Responsible Investing (SRI) in Hedge Funds:

◈ **SRI Principles:** As the world increasingly prioritizes environmental, social, and governance (ESG) considerations, hedge funds must align their strategies with these principles. We delve into the ethical imperative of responsible investing and the ways in which hedge funds can integrate ESG factors into their decision-making.

◈ **ESG Integration:** Ethical investing goes beyond financial returns; it incorporates social and environmental impacts. We explore the integration of ESG factors into hedge fund investment decisions, emphasizing the moral imperatives of responsible investing.

5. Transparency and Investor Relations in Hedge Funds:

⟐ **Transparency Requirements:** We scrutinize the ethical obligation of hedge funds to provide transparency to investors. This includes not only financial reporting but also fee disclosures, risk communication, and open and honest dialogue with investors.

⟐ **Investor Relations:** Ethical investor relations go beyond compliance. We examine the ethical aspects of treating investors fairly, disclosing conflicts of interest, and clearly communicating fund performance.

6. Ethical Dilemmas and Case Studies:

⟐ **Case Studies:** To illuminate the complexities of ethical decision-making in the hedge fund world, we present real-world case studies. These case studies highlight the ethical dilemmas that hedge funds have faced and the critical choices they made. Through these scenarios, we underscore the importance of ethical reflection and decision-making frameworks.

⟐ **Ethical Decision Framework:** We provide guidance on ethical decision-making by introducing practical frameworks that hedge fund managers can employ when navigating challenging ethical dilemmas. These frameworks help hedge funds maintain their integrity and reputation.

7. **Regulatory and Compliance Framework:**

⟐ **Regulatory Compliance:** We emphasize the alignment of ethical standards with regulatory requirements. It's not just about adhering to the law; it's about exceeding the minimum standards and demonstrating a commitment to ethical behavior.

⟐ **Ethics and Regulatory Oversight:** We explore the critical role played by regulatory authorities in enforcing ethical standards and monitoring compliance within the hedge fund industry. Regulatory oversight serves as an external check on ethical conduct.

8. Future Trends and Emerging Ethical Issues:

◈ **Emerging Ethical Challenges:** As the financial landscape evolves, new ethical challenges arise. We delve into these emerging ethical issues, such as evolving regulations, global ethical considerations, and the ethical implications of rapidly advancing technology. Staying ahead of these issues is key to ethical leadership in the industry.

Don't miss out!

Visit the website below and you can sign up to receive emails whenever Alex Thompson publishes a new book. There's no charge and no obligation.

https://books2read.com/r/B-A-FEPY-JPTOC

BOOKS 2 READ

Connecting independent readers to independent writers.

Also by Alex Thompson

Alex on Finance

Financial Freedom Roadmap - Achieving Early Retirement through the FIRE Movement
The Art of Strategic Innovation
Beyond Cash - The Evolution of Digital Payment Systems and the Future of Money
Preserving Wealth in Inflationary Times - Strategies for Protecting Your Financial Future

Standalone

Side Hustle Success: Unlocking Your Entrepreneurial Potential
Side Hustle Success: The Ultimate Guide to Passive and Financial Freedom
Mastering the Markets: Advanced Trading Strategies for Success and Ethical Trading Practices
Financial Fortitude
Mastering the Art of Upselling
The Financial Bullet Blueprint
Investing Demystified: A Beginner's Guide to Building Wealth in the Stock Market
Real Estate Riches: Building Wealth through Property Investment
How To Succeed as a Freelancer

Navigating Complex Waters: Advanced Strategies in Portfolio Management
Behavioral Finance and Investor Psychology
Leading with Empathy: Harnessing Emotional Intelligence for Effective Leadership
Financial Independence
Thriving Within Your Means: A Guide to Affordable Living
Algorithmic Trading: Navigating the Digital Frontier
Navigating Alternative Investments
Navigating the Behavioral Finance Landscape
Unlocking the Power of Derivatives
Mastering International Finance
Quantitative Finance and Risk Modeling
Sustainable and ESG Investing
Derivatives Dynamics: Navigating Risk and Innovation
Options Mastery: Navigating the Financial Frontier
Portfolio Mastery: Navigating the Financial Art and Science
Ethics in Hedge Funds: Navigating the Moral Compass of Finance
Structured Finance: Navigating Innovation, Sustainability and Ethics

www.ingramcontent.com/pod-product-compliance
Lightning Source LLC
LaVergne TN
LVHW022056200926
848481LV00003B/933